Making Party Decorations and Crackers

Making
Party Decorations
and
Crackers

Pamela Woods

with drawings and photographs
by Michael Woods

Blandford Press   London

A021250

This book was designed and produced by
Alphabet and Image, Sherborne, Dorset.

First published by Blandford Press Ltd 1974

Typeset by Specialised Offset Services Ltd, Liverpool
Printed and bound in Great Britain by Redwood Burn Ltd,
Trowbridge & Esher

ISBN: 0 7137 0694 5

Contents

Acknowledgments

It was my mother who made the first party decorations I ever saw. It was from her that I learned, a little later, the practical skills of making crackers and using display materials. It is her own high standards in the art of decoration that I regard as my touchstone for my own work, and in assessing this book she will be my most stern and valued critic.

The history of decorations is widely studied and widely documented, but in the rather specialized field of Christmas crackers my research into their history has been greatly aided by the generous help of the staff of Tom Smith & Co. Ltd of Norwich, with whose help I was able to trace the development of crackers from Victorian times to the present day.

1 It's Your Party

A party is a personal thing. Most party-givers know exactly what sort of party they want, and after it is over there is usually little doubt about its success, or its failure.

It is certainly not the aim of this book to organize or to prompt hosts and hostesses, for it is a practical book of ideas for making and decorating. It will be of little use to those who prefer their party surroundings to be stark, or dark, but hopefully it will help those who are prepared to spend a little time setting the scene, and who think, as I do, that surroundings can contribute to or detract from the party atmosphere.

The planning of your party is as important, if not more so, than anything you may do during it. A relaxed hostess owes her success to careful and considered planning beforehand not only in the choice of food and decorations but also the amount of time she spends on them. It is a great shame to waste your particular talents by having to throw together make-do decorations simply because time has run out, and as most of them will be made of paper or dried plant materials they can be prepared well in advance and then stored away while you prepare the food. Decorations for a party have a life of only one evening so you should limit preparation time accordingly. At the same time, do not feel that a decoration that may have taken many hours to make *has* to be thrown away after the party. In particular, some Christmas tree designs can be made for re-use in subsequent years. In my family we make one new Christmas tree decoration every year and our collection is now quite large (and even includes some kept by my Grandmother).

Crackers, of course, are entirely different because they are made to be destroyed. To spend a great deal of time making them is a waste. Though this book contains cracker designs of all types, try to be ingenious in the use of exciting and unusual papers for the basic crackers rather than spending hours making decorations for them.

Expense by no means ensures the success of your decorations; in fact clever economy of material and simplicity of design can produce more impact than an extravagant and costly display. The colour scheme you choose should extend to as many areas of your decorations as possible, particularly in the same room. The repetition of one motif several times can be effective too. Your decorations are there primarily to create a party atmosphere and only secondarily as a source of conversation for your guests. For the normal gathering in an average home, an expensive display is more likely to put a damper on the spirits than to make your guests relax. You should try to make something witty or graceful, but above all, inventive. Remember, too, that your guests are the real stars of the occasion, or at least they should feel they are.

Deciding the positions of your decorations is another aspect to consider. For a drinks or buffet party where your guests are to remain standing, remember that nothing will be seen below a height of about four feet, so place your decorations high — on the mantlepiece, on a tall piece of furniture or on the wall. Make sure that wherever you put your displays they are stable, so that you do not put your guests into the embarrassing position of knocking half your decorations over.

The following chapters include various suggestions for decorating walls and tables and for wrapping presents attractively, as well as for making a wide range of crackers. I hope you will find many that will interest you and that you will be inspired to make other designs of your own.

2 Decorations to Hang

A door decoration, however simple, is itself a good start to your party. The entrance door is of course the most important one to decorate, but inside the house, if you are using more than one room for your party, you can decorate the doors of the different rooms, and also you can make attractive the naming of the bathroom, cloakroom, etc, in a similar way.

An outside door must have a weather-proof decoration. Papers which lose their colour as well as their shape when wet will make a very sorry display, and are useless there, and anything which is fragile enough to be spoilt in the wind is best avoided. Try using acetate film or Melinex foil for stars and flowers, or glass balls attached with wire to a central hanger. Make use of a door knob as an attachment point, but do not hang it so close that it is impossible for a visitor to knock on or open your door without getting pricked or knocking off your decoration. If there is nothing on the surface of the door, you can make a wire hook to go over the top of the door, rather like a picture hook. Make sure that whatever you hang the decoration by is strong enough to hold the display, and do not underestimate its weight.

A centrally-placed letter slot can be useful in holding your decoration in place, with strings to the inside of the door, although of course a long-stay decoration held in such a way would confound the Christmas postman.

The custom of hanging a decorative wreath on the door at Christmas is widespread, and it is interesting to experiment with your own designs. Try using ivy, plain or variegated, and small conifer branches as well as holly, and add glass or, better still, unbreakable coloured plastic balls. The display shown on page 11 is a spray of different kinds of ivy, hung with cones of silver foil. Some of the cones are made into a star whilst the others are threaded on to silver strings so that they constantly move and glitter in the wind.

If you prefer a more formal type of decoration a tight spray of flowers, leaves, fircones and ribbon can be wired together, and you should aim to make a tall shape which matches the shape of the door.

Ceilings and Walls

Apart from the door, hanging decorations are either free-hanging from the ceiling or attached to a wall. Try to avoid the pitfalls of hanging your decoration just where the heads of your taller guests may hit it — free-hanging designs are only satisfactory if your rooms are high enough to give plenty of headroom below them. The materials you use should not be too heavy, but there is a wide variety to choose from, both artificial and natural.

If you are lucky enough to have a room with open rafters, these form an excellent framework from which to hang decorations, either artificial or natural. Seed heads hung down by their stalks can look quite spectacular, and if you can not find this sort of natural decoration you can suspend flower balls made according to the following instructions.

The Flower Ball

This is a very simple decoration to make, using an Oasis ball as the foundation. Thread a cord or ribbon through the ball with a big needle, tying it on the underside, to make the hanger. Then add paper flowers, dried grasses, nuts or seed heads by pushing

fig. 1   *The Flower Ball*

their stems into the ball, like pins into a pincushion, strengthening them if necessary with florist's wire. Try to keep the ball hanging vertically by arranging the flowers symmetrically and keeping the weight evenly balanced. The success of this sort of decoration depends largely on the colour scheme you choose. Use two or three main colours, not more, and if you make several balls of this kind, keep the colour schemes the same throughout, though you can vary the size of the balls. At Christmas, you can adapt this to become a festive ball of mistletoe, with holly and small bows of coloured ribbon.

Frilly Paper Balls

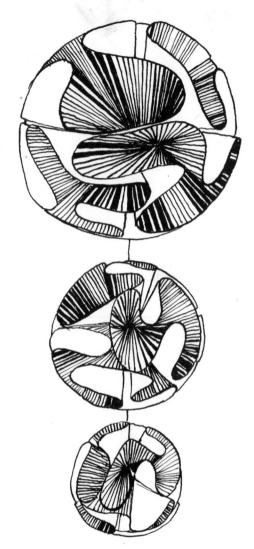

Fig. 2 shows a different type of ball, made very simply using just thin Melinex foil. Balls can be made in different sizes and suspended in families, as shown here. You will need thin Melinex (or a substitute such as coloured tissue paper), some paper the thickness of postcard, a small stapler and scissors.

Cut eight circles of equal size from the Melinex and two smaller circles out of the stiff card. If you use a milk bottle or a jam jar as a pattern for the Melinex circles, then the card circle should be about ½ inch (1.3 cm) across. Fold each of the Melinex circles loosely in half, and ease each side into the fold as shown in fig. 3. Be careful not to crease the paper as this will remove the 'spring' which gives shape to the flower. Now staple the folded circle to one of the card circles (fig. 4). Four such shapes fit on to the circle as shown in fig. 5. When you have reached this stage you have completed half the ball, and the shapes will spring upwards to make a hemispherical form.

Repeat this with the other four Melinex circles and the other card circle, and complete the ball by stapling the two cards together, taking care not to damage or staple the frills.

If you want to hang the ball by a single thread place fine cotton or transparent fishing line between the cards before you staple them together, and you can thus make an 'invisible' suspender.

fig. 2

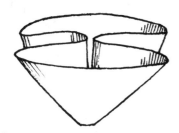

fig. 3

fig. 4

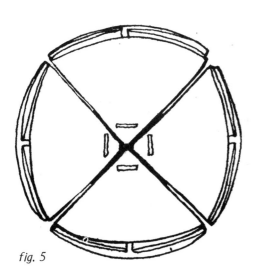

fig. 5

Frilly balls of this kind are quick to make and can be any size. A popular and colourful version is made by making each folded frill out of two circles of paper of contrasting colours. If this two-toned ball is made in contrasting Melinex the two colours reflect each other.

Complete balls look their best when hung, but if you wish the hemispherical half-made ball can be used on a flat surface, or even on a parcel, like a rose or a ribbon bow (see page 97).

Mobiles

Most things that are suspended hang straight downwards, but you can use balance to modify gravity by making mobile decorations with arms of thin wire arranged horizontally. To make a successful mobile for a party, something fairly spectacular has to be suspended from the arms, and one suggestion is gaily coloured paper butterflies which, because of the resistance of their large wings to currents of air, will be constantly moving.

You will need milliner's wire, binding wire, narrow cellulose tape (scotch tape or Sellotape), five wooden beads for each butterfly, scissors, glue and a material for covering the butterflies' wings. This can be any kind of paper or foil which is light in weight, and the material I have found the most spectacular is perforated sequin ribbon (see page 48) — foil punched with round holes — which prevents the butterfly from looking too solid.

The butterfly frame is made from a continuous piece of milliner's wire, as shown in fig. 6. First make a double loop as in **a**, binding the join with tape. You have thus made the front pair of wings, and should continue to make two more, but smaller, loops for the hind pair of wings, cutting off the spare wire when the shape is complete, and binding again with a short piece of tape (**b**) before securing the central cross with binding wire. Squeeze each loop into a pointed shape (**c**) and apply glue to the whole of one side of the wire frame. The frame can now be pressed firmly on to the paper or foil you have chosen for the wings, and when it is quite dry cut round the outer edge of the frame as closely as possible to the wire so that no paper overlaps. It is not necessary to fold the paper over the wire.

To make the body of the butterfly, take a piece of binding wire and bend it (**d**) with a kink near the bend to hold the beads in place. Thread the five beads on to the double wire from the 'antennae' end before curling the projecting ends of wire into a spiral as shown in **e**. Join the body to the underside of the wings with a piece of binding wire, leaving a long end with which to hang it. The wings can be eased upwards to make the creature more life-like (**f**) and any necessary adjustments can be made to perfect the balance by altering the angle of the butterfly itself.

You will note that I have given no measurements in these instructions, for the size of the butterflies can vary according to taste, and provided that the proportions are kept constant. It is worth experimenting with several different materials to make the wings. Japanese lacy paper, Cellophane or cellulose film, foil and coloured acetate are all suitable. Butterflies with silver Melinex wings will rotate in the warm air and send reflections around a room.

Five or six butterflies of varying size look well on a mobile if the wire hangers are kept thin and the thread is nearly invisible, and personally I think they look best if they all have the same colour of wings. Try to suspend your butterflies at different heights to prevent them colliding.

A single butterfly suspended by a thread from the ceiling can look most impressive, especially if it is large — up to two feet (60 cm) across. If you make really large butterflies you will need to use silk-covered Christmas balls instead of beads for the body, and milliner's wire for the antennae.

Tree Decorations

At Christmas time, a tree, real or artificial, is usually the centre of attention and, alas, it is so often badly decorated. Heavy

14

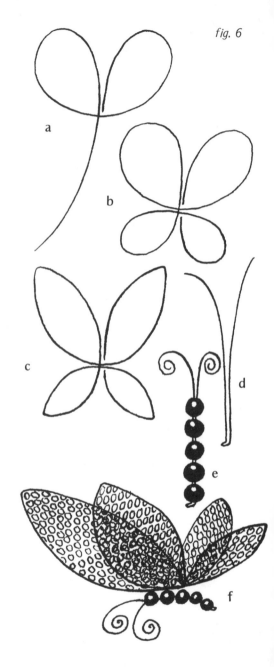

fig. 6

fig. 7

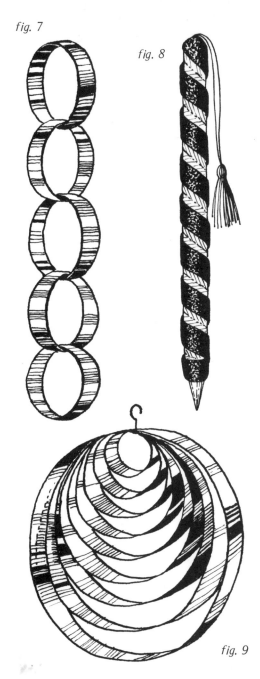

fig. 8

parcels weighing down branches or swathes of paper tissue and electrical flex do their best to hide or distort the natural form of the tree, which is in fact ideally suited for pendant decorations.

A large range of hanging balls and stars is always available at Christmas, but it is often more satisfying to make your own. Keep them simple, and use repeating hanging shapes wherever possible. With a stapler and foil strips you can quickly make linked chains, rings, or rings-within-rings, as shown in fig. 9, and for a change make miniature chains to hang vertically on the tree rather than in festoons. The natural springiness of thin Melinex will keep shapes like these crisp and alive.

Lightweight satin-covered balls can be decorated with lace, beads and sequins secured with pins, as shown in fig. 10. Pencils or ball-point pens can be covered with velvet ribbon and gold cord wrapped into a spiral, like the stripes on a barber's pole (fig. 8). Put a tassel and a loop made of the cord on each so that they can be attached to the tree like icicles. These long thin shapes are a welcome change from the more usual rounded forms of tree decoration.

fig. 9

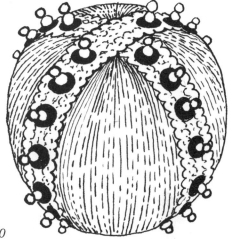

fig. 10

The Festoon

Where hanging decorations are attached to the wall, they are often used to surround a more permanent fixture like a mirror, a doorway or a picture, or are themselves the feature of an otherwise plain wall. The secret of making a successful ornamental surround is to use a foundation of something fairly rigid, such as galvanized wire, to which leaves, flowers, papers, ribbons, tinsels, balls or the inevitable Christmas holly can be bound, to give strength. Fig. 11 shows such a design in which a wire hook at each end is covered with decorations including six paper lilies, holly and two streamers of ribbon. The 'horizontal' part of the design should be curved to create a natural and attractive effect.

Decorated Panel

Fig. 12 shows quite a different type of wall hanging. The base panel is made of cardboard covered with flocked paper, but it can be made of any stout material or coloured card. Dried plants, fircones and foil flowers are arranged attractively and bound together with wire. Ornamental feathers (parts of peacock tail feathers which can be bought in many florist's

fig. 11

16

shops) are included in the design illustrated here, and the spray is held in place on the panel by making a central hole through which the binding wire is passed and splayed out on the back.

It is important to remember that the backing material must be strong enough to support your design — thin paper or cotton material is too flimsy, and although the colour can be strong it must be unpatterned and should contrast in tone and texture with the display you put on it.

A bamboo cane with a cord to a convenient attachment point on the wall is a decorative way of hanging the panel. Alternatively, the ends of wire behind the panel can be twisted together to form a concealed hook.

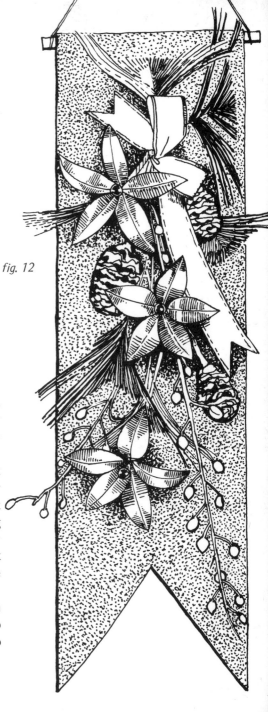

fig. 12

Wall Flowers

Fig. 13 shows a mixture of dried and artificial flowers as a wall decoration, without a background panel. The basis of the arrangement is a lightweight Oasis block, which is secured to the wall simply by being pushed on to a nail. The flowers form a dense display, completely hiding the Oasis into which their stems are inserted. You will see that the pattern made by the flowers radiates from the centre, and the large and solid items — crepe paper roses and carnations made from pheasant feathers bound to wire stems with Gutta Percha (see Chapter 9) — are kept near the focus of attention, while the small soft hare's-tails are arranged around the edges. Try to avoid using materials which will shed seeds or petals on the floor — gravity is against you when you make a wall panel or spray — but do not be afraid of using really strong colour schemes — I made the one shown here in gold, yellow and orange.

Your wall hanging, whatever form it takes, may be taken down the day after the party but the nail which has held it to the wall will leave its mark. Before you make decorations to

fig. 13

hang on the wall, therefore, it is a good idea to spend a little time working out how they can hang safely without leaving scars. One solution, if no-one objects, is to take down pictures before a party, and borrow their hooks for your temporary decoration.

3 Decorations for the Table

At a party, the place of prime importance is nearly always the table and it should, therefore, be suitably decorated. Whether guests are to sit down to dine or to stand at a buffet party the table will almost certainly be covered with food, as well as your decorations, so they should be complementary.

The size of your table decorations is very important, and they must not be allowed to stray into the food or get in the way of serving dishes. Make your dinner table displays as low as possible, so that your guests do not have to peer at each other through a jungle of flowers and ribbons. If space on the table is limited make your arrangement on top of some sort of pedestal, to free the area on the table which would have been covered by your flowers. The gold and silver flowers in Plate 1 are arranged in a piece of Oasis wired to a brass candlestick. If, however, you have a large table, it will look better with two identical arrangements placed one near each end rather than an over-large central one.

The qualities of candlelight, and the atmosphere that candles can create, are now fully appreciated, and there is almost no limit to the colour, shape and size of candles which can now be bought or made. Keep the general colour scheme of your table or room in mind when choosing coloured candles, and remember that candle flames can and do set light to decorations all too easily. It is the height of the candle flame which is

fig. 14

significant, and you can safely group paper decorations below the level of the candle, but not alongside it. Wide slow-burning candles are excellent for parties — never the very thin ones because they burn down far too quickly. Fig. 14 shows how a striking table centre can be made around just one fat candle, using a cardboard cake stand as a base.

Cone Candle Stand

You will need half a yard (45 cm) of Melinex, 24 inches (61 cm) wide, foil or other shiny material, as well as a cardboard cake stand, glue, a stapler and a candle.

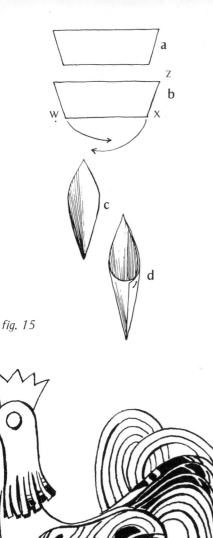

fig. 15

fig. 16

y The spiky cones are made out of boat-shaped pieces of Melinex (a), and the number you will require depends on the size of the candle and the cake stand — forty-seven cones were used in the design illustrated. Cut about forty-seven shapes as in a with sides 6½ and 5 inches (16.5 and 12.5 cm) long and 2½ inches (6 cm) deep. Holding one shape by its shorter side wx, curve it round so that w and x overlap each other (b), and y and z coincide to make a point. Then staple the cone shape together as shown in c, placing the staple as far as possible inside the cone (d). Cover the base board with material (the same material you have used for the cones is best) and glue on a second row of about sixteen cones, rather closer to the centre. Now place the candle in the exact centre. You may not be able to glue the candle in position, but Plasticine or Oasis Fix will prevent it from sliding or falling. For the third ring you will need about eleven cones, the closed ends of which should touch the candle, but do not try to force in more units than are necessary to make a complete circle.

Material which has two different-coloured surfaces is very suitable for this design because both colours are revealed by the curvature of the cones. The same effect can be achieved by using two papers back to back. Another useful material is wide florist's ribbon.

Animals and Birds

Acetate and Melinex are excellent materials to use for making decorations which are required to stand with no support. Stylized birds and animals to decorate a children's party table can be made quickly and the cockerel shown in fig. 16 is one such example in which several layers of acetate, and trimmings of Melinex, are combined. The foot is also made with several layers which, when joined at the heel, will fan out to give the bird stability.

21

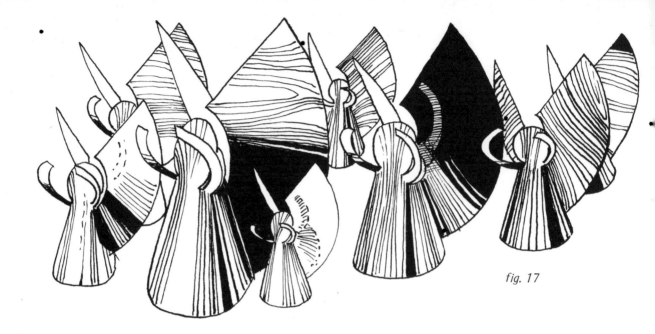

fig. 17

Silver Angels

A great many of the most effective decorations are built from simple units which children can make. At Christmas time the simplicity of silver foil angels is a welcome contrast to other decorations. When made in different sizes and grouped together they seem to acquire personalities of their own. They stand up easily and can be arranged and rearranged without protesting. By simply unfastening them they can be stored flat in an envelope until they are needed again.

For one angel you will need a circle of silver Melinex about 3 inches (7.5 cm) in diameter and a pair of scissors. It is important to follow the diagram alongside exactly when cutting the foil. Each line on the diagram represents a cut. The horseshoe shape in the centre of the circle makes the arms of the angel, and the head is the central disk (x). Note carefully the two slots a and b because the placing of these ensures the stability of the angel. When you have cut the foil as shown, curl

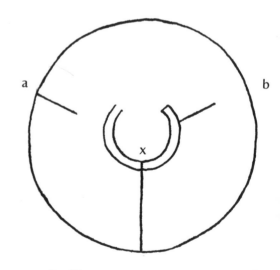

fig. 18

the whole shape round and overlap the ends until slot **b** corresponds with slot **a**. Simply slot one into the other and crease the arms at the shoulder point so that they cross over in front. Fig. 17 shows a host of angels.

Natural Painted Arrangements

Fresh flowers are sometimes a luxury, but you may well feel that as your party is a special occasion you should not be without them. You can economize when flowers are expensive, as in winter, by buying only a few and enriching your arrangement with some fresh or dried fruit sprayed gold with an aerosol paint spray. This may seem tragically wasteful, but the very small amount of fruit you will need will almost certainly be much cheaper than the flowers, and you can always spray for decoration fruit which is not suitable for eating.

Great care must be taken with the aerosol paint because the spray tends to drift on to the furniture, so make sure your working surface is well covered by newspaper or sheeting which should extend far beyond the actual material you have to spray. I prefer to use polythene to be sure that no paint penetrates to the table below. The ideal place for spraying is a garage or garden shed where drifting spray cannot cause much damage. Whatever you spray should have a thorough and even coat: nothing in decoration is successful if it is halfhearted. Only natural forms with a clearly defined and fairly regular shape look well under a coat of gold paint.

page 34

Plate 2 shows a fruit and flower display arranged on a copper tray. To achieve the effect of a heap of fruit the items are arranged in a piece of Oasis, and rich dark green ivy is used to give contrast. The foliage provides the background for the spray of chrysanthemums which are separated and the flowers individually wired. The fruit is a mixture: there are two apples, an ornamental gourd, a very small bunch of twelve grapes and a few of last year's nuts, all of which are sprayed gold. The final addition of green velvet ribbon adds a rich contrast in texture.

23

4　The Basic Cracker

The Christmas cracker, or 'party favor' as it is called in America, is a spectacular form of gift wrapping. The basic cylindrical shape is both traditional and symbolic and the cracker outline is so readily recognizable that it conveys a Christmas message on posters and cards without the need for any wording.

Crackers are made today by the same method as was used last century: a flat piece of paper is rolled around a tube. Though often disguised with frilled papers and central motifs, the unit is this hollow tube of paper and card which is constricted at two points along its length by creases or 'chokes' left when a piece of string is twisted round it and then released. This sufficiently seals the centre part so that the gift does not fall out. Lying inside the tube, and for almost all its length, is the snap or 'banger' which gives the cracker its name. Saltpetre lying on an area of friction between two strips of card should be enough to cause the minute explosion when the cracker is pulled. The ends of the snap must be accessible and easy to grasp — it is disappointing when it fails to go off.

In addition to the snap, you will need strong string, glue, scissors, lining paper about the thickness of tissue paper, card about the thickness of the card used to make cereal packets, covering paper (the range of decorative papers is very varied and is described in Chapter 5), the gift or 'filling' (suggestions for gifts will be found in Chapter 5) and 'formers' or shapers, usually made of metal, around which the paper is rolled and which prevent the cracker from being squashed when the string is twisted to form the creases, or 'chokes'.

It is possible to buy, from the sources indicated on page 100, the basic tools for cracker-making. The formers are two hollow light metal tubes with the same diameters but different lengths. These pairs of tubes normally come in two sizes, sold as sizes 4 and 5. Size 4 makes a cracker 8¾ inches (22 cm) long, and the tubes measure 8 inches (20 cm) and 4 inches (10 cm) long and are $1\frac{3}{8}$ inches (3.5 cm) in diameter. Size 5 makes a larger cracker, 10 inches (25 cm) long, and the tubes are 10 inches (25 cm) and 5 inches (12.5 cm) long, by 1½ inches (3.7 cm) across. If you are unable or unwilling to buy these cracker-making tubes or formers, you can be encouraged by the fact that there are dozens of acceptable substitutes. The best one I know is the grey plastic piping which is used for kitchen and bathroom sinks, available by the foot from all plumbers and most hardware shops. Another alternative is aluminium tubing produced for television aerials.

However elaborate you may wish to make the cracker, you will start with the following sequence, which is for the basic cracker before any kind of decoration is added.

Before you begin, make yourself a measurement card or plan, and mark it as shown on pages 28-9. You can trace this diagram and then transfer the measurements on to a thickish piece of light card. You will use this plan again and again, and as it will get the odd drop of glue and colour from your paper, it is not advisable to use the one in the book itself as your plan. The instructions which follow and the plan on pages 28-9 are for the larger, size 5, cracker, and if you use a smaller former for smaller crackers, you must reduce the plan in proportion.

What you need to make one cracker

A piece of single crepe paper 12 x 6¾ inches (30.5 x 17 cm), with the grain running the *length* of the paper. (If the grain

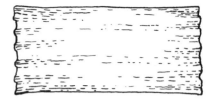

fig. 19

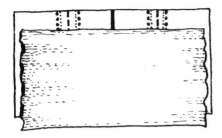

fig. 20

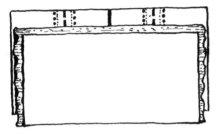

fig. 21

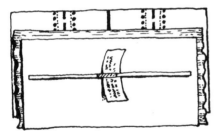

fig. 22

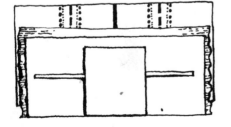

fig. 23

runs in the wrong direction you will have difficulty in pulling the cracker.)

A piece of lining paper 11 x 6 inches (28 x 15 cm).

A snap. Snaps can be bought in quantity from the sources given on page 100.

A motto or a message — optional but can be amusing.

A piece of stiffening card 6 x 3½ inches (15 x 9 cm).

The filling (there is a host of suggestions on pages 39-41).

Tools

A pair of formers, size 5.

A piece of strong string for making the chokes. One end of this should be firmly anchored, for example to a table leg on the side of the table furthest away from you.

Glue (any clear impact adhesive such as Uhu will do).

What to do

1. Take the piece of crepe paper and make a frill all across both ends by lightly stretching it between fingers and thumbs in a series of movements along the edge (fig. 19).

2. Lay the crepe paper on the plan (fig. 20) and then place the lining paper on top of it, making sure that the two edges nearest you are together (fig. 21) and that you can just see the card at the far edge. The crepe paper, being larger than the lining paper, is visible along the top and at both ends.

3. Now place the snap and motto (if you want one) on top (fig. 22) and put the stiffening card in position in the centre, lining it up with former lines 2 and 3 on the plan, as shown in fig. 24. Notice that the stiffener runs at right angles to the other materials, not in the same direction.

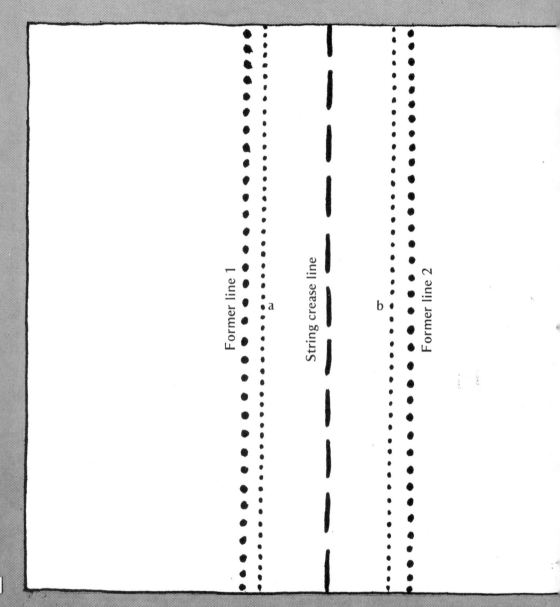

Former line 1

String crease line

Former line 2

a

b

fig. 24 Cracker plan

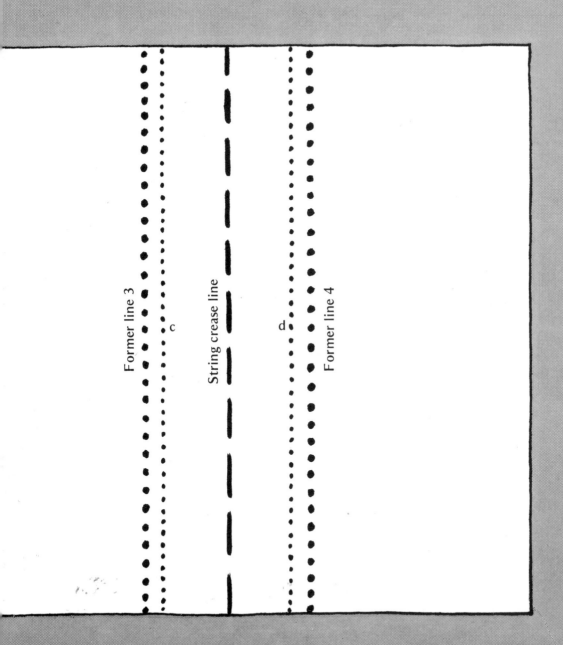

Former line 3

c

String crease line

d

Former line 4

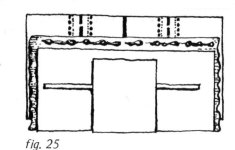

fig. 25

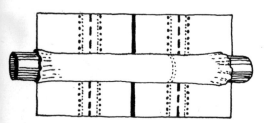

fig. 26

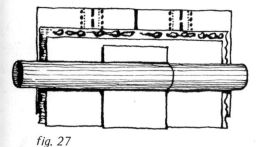

fig. 27

fig. 28

4. Apply a light coating of glue along the length of the crepe paper visible at the top (fig. 25).

5. Place the larger former on the stiffener card so that one end is exactly level with the edge of the stiffener card on former line 3, and about 1 inch (2.5 cm) in from the edge of the paper nearest to you (fig. 26). Then put the other former on to the paper so that it touches the first one and forms a continuous tube (fig. 27).

6. Holding the two formers in place, lift up the edge of the crepe paper nearest to you, roll it over the formers and then continue rolling it all away from you, keeping the paper pressed tightly to the formers so that they stay in line and do not separate. When you reach the far, glued, edge of the paper, press down on the roll and hold it for a moment to ensure that the glue sticks firmly. Move the whole roll a little to the right, feel for the joint between the formers and align this joint with former line **c** on the plan (fig. 28).

7. Ease the short former away from the big one until it reaches former line **d** (fig. 29).

8. Holding both formers with one hand, pull the free end of the string towards you, over the top of the cracker, back beneath it and over the top again towards you (fig. 30).

9. Make sure that the string is lying on the string-crease line on the plan, and then pull it tight. It is important that you hold both formers with your left hand with the string passing between your fingers. You will feel the formers coming together. To ensure an even crease on the cracker you must make sure that the strain is made equally from both sides, by pulling the cracker away from the anchored end and towards you at the same time as you pull the string. With a little more practice you will find that you constrict the paper evenly and make a professional choke on the cracker.

10. Now press the two formers back together again and give

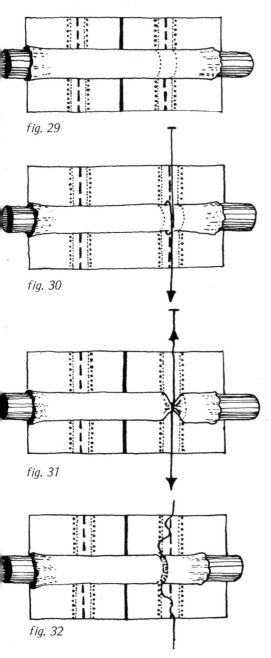

fig. 29

fig. 30

fig. 31

fig. 32

them a little twist. This creases the crepe paper and crispens the outline. Release the string and remove the smaller former. Do not let the large former come out at this stage, as it is almost impossible to get it back in again if you do.

11. Lift up the cracker, drop in the filling through the centre of the large former, and ease the former out a little way to ensure your filling has not stuck to it. Then replace the cracker on the plan. Slide the former outwards until it reaches former line **a** (fig. 33), again making sure that the filling does not come with it. The edge of the centre part of the cracker, which is now only held in shaped by the stiffening card, should lie on former line **b**.

12. Twist the string round the cracker as before. Press the former towards the centre to close up the gap and then remove it. This last stage is made with the support removed from the central part of the cracker, and it must be done carefully but confidently, so that the cylindrical shape of the cracker is not lost. Your basic cracker is now completed.

Common Faults

Things often go wrong when you are beginning. Here are a few tips to help you to avoid mistakes.

1. If the line of the cracker is crooked it is because the string twisted into a spiral instead of following the string-crease line

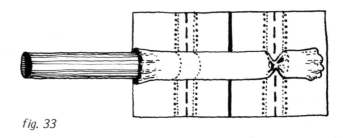

fig. 33

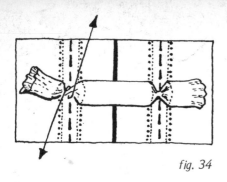

fig. 34

exactly on both sides of the cracker when you pulled it (fig. 34).

2. If the outline is not as crisp as it should be, it is probably because you have pulled the formers too far apart when making the crease.

3. If the cracker is loose and untidy, the fault can be avoided in the future by rolling the papers much more tightly before glueing.

Lining the ends

To enable your crackers to stand up to the closest scrutiny, you may like to make this small modification.

Cut your crepe paper 16 x 6¾ inches (40.5 x 17 cm) instead of 12 x 6¾ inches (30.5 x 17 cm), and lay it on the plan as usual. Put the lining paper and the snap on it and *fold over* the ends of the crepe paper for 2 inches (5 cm) at each end. You can still frill the double layer of crepe which now forms the ends of your paper. Proceed to make the cracker as already described. When the cracker is completed, the hollow ends will be lined with the crepe paper, and the lining paper will be hidden.

Choice of decoration

You can now add decorations if you wish, although if you have chosen an interesting paper you may feel no need to add anything at all.

The wide choice of papers and decorations available means that your crackers can be adapted to suit any occasion, from christenings to anniversaries, children's parties, dinner parties, and any gathering where their cheerful presence would be an asset. Crackers are ice-breakers at parties, and if you make and fill them with your particular guests in mind they are certain to arouse surprise and delight. In the following chapters I will describe some of the variations possible on such occasions.

Plate 1 Gold and silver foil crackers with a matching flower decoration graces a festive table. Use silver foil to cover table mats to complete the scheme.

5 The Paper and the Contents

It was about the year 1840 that Tom Smith, a London sweet and pastry shop owner, made a memorable trip to Paris. There he saw sweets elegantly wrapped in paper twisted at both ends. He was looking at bon-bons, inventively wrapped with the flair the French have always shown.

He decided to copy the idea, and then to improve upon it. He included love messages in the wrappings and called them 'kiss mottoes'. The story goes that it was the sound of crackling logs which inspired him to put a cracker into his bon-bon, and he spent two years devising, with explosives including saltpetre, a harmless friction strip of paper which would nevertheless go off with a loud report when torn apart, and thus, over a century ago, the cracker was invented and named. By late Victorian times the contents included a range of novelty gifts as well as confectionery and they were sometimes called 'bangs of expectation'. Characteristic of their age, they were ornate, with long skirts and frills, and contrasted a uniform exterior with variety within. To the Victorians, crackers were far from the rather childish amusement they have sometimes become today, and the clever hostess would produce her box of crackers during a lull in the conversation at her dinner party.

By this time Tom Smith was manufacturing crackers in vast numbers, and a catalogue of the products of his factory in 1899 is a document of social history. 'Curios from the Klondyke',

Plate 2 At the heart of this table decoration is an Oasis block which keeps the flowers and fruit in place. See page 23.

'Japanese Gardens' and 'Nansen's Trip to the North Pole' were some of the themes for boxes of crackers, just as an Apollo moonflight is celebrated on children's games today. The boxes, verses, mottoes and filling were all designed to a common theme, and treasures collected from crackers would be stuck into scrap books. The photograph opposite shows a 'snapshot box' of 1900 in which the ends of the box are made to resemble a camera, and the crackers contain miniature peepshows and photo albums. A box of crackers of this early date is a rare item indeed today, for crackers were made to be destroyed and very few can have survived.

Factory-made crackers have continued to use themes for their decoration and their contents, and the contents conform to the formula paper-hat-plus-small-gift-plus-motto. 'Motto' is indeed the name for the written content but it is more usually a pale joke than a verse of love. The cracker manufacturer does not have the advantage of knowing your guests, and you must not waste this advantage. You can buy paper hats or even printed mottoes if you wish, and put them inside the cracker with the gift, but you can include messages to suit your guests, or link your dinner guests with the clues of a game.

The gifts themselves, of course, should be a pleasure to devise and not a boring chore. Provided the contents are not dangerously sharp, highly inflammable, poisonous or too fragile, the only restriction on what goes inside a cracker is one of size — it must fit into the central portion of the cylinder. This varies in size in proportion to the cracker itself, and can be quite tiny, or big enough to hold a live bunny girl for the truly expansive.

Without straying beyond the normal dimensions of a cracker (the central compartment is up to 5 inches (12.5 cm) long and 1½ inches (3.7 cm) wide) the range of gifts or fillings is enormous. It is important to avoid the mistake of lavishing so much attention on the paper and the design of the cracker that the contents come as a disappointment, and for this reason I am describing the contents before the packaging.

Victorian delights revealed in the 'Snapshot Box': crackers made in 1900.

Huge exploding crackers with people inside are a familiar feature of the theatre and the fancy dress ball. One Victorian baronet is said to have commissioned a thirty-foot cracker to be built, with a spiral staircase inside, around one of the pillars in his ballroom. His cracker was detonated so that it exploded with coloured fires, showering gifts, and at the same time lighting festoons of coloured lights.

It is not always size which has distinguished the extravagant and eccentric cracker. A box of crackers costing hundreds of pounds was a bridegroom's gift to the bridesmaids at his wedding. Each cracker was wrapped in figured satin and edged with old lace. Octagonal caskets formed the centres, and in each one a tiny key unlocked a silver door to reveal a gift of jewelry inside. An even more expensive cracker, which took six months to make, at a cost of £4,000, was only four inches long, but was made from solid gold and contained a ring of rare pearls.

The most inventive cracker I have ever heard of, however, was a leap-year cracker sent by a lady, which contained not only a proposal of marriage but other necessities too: an engagement ring, wedding ring, marriage licence and certificate.

The cost of the contents depends on you, and can be very little. A teabag or a clothes peg is not only cheap but worth keeping and using, whilst cigarette lighters, jewelry, even a diamond-studded watch, will fit in the space available. If you are in doubt about the maximum size for a filling, take one of the formers with you on a shopping expedition so that you can be sure that everything you buy will fit.

I have made a list of a few hundred suggestions for gifts, grouped according to the shops in which they are most likely to be found. I am sure you will be able to add to this list easily, across a wide range of prices. If you are making crackers for children try to keep the values of the gifts even, to avoid disappointment, and to escape the embarrassment of giving adults toys meant for children make two different colours or designs so that crackers can be appropriately placed around the table or handed out without revealing their contents.

If you run out of ideas, then cracker fillings can be bought ready selected from cracker suppliers (see page 100), together with paper hats neatly and tightly rolled.

If your choice for a filling consists of several units (like a handful of marbles) it is a good idea to pre-package your gift so that it is a compact shape when it goes into the cracker, and remember that it should not be too small in diameter, or it can fall out through one of the ends ahead of its time. If you want to include very small gifts, such as sparklers, fix them to the paper hat by its rubber band.

Gifts and fillings

Chemists and drugstores

Soap, bath salts, bubble bath sachet, shampoo, perfume, tissues, cotton wool, hair pins, paper pants, hand cream, flannel, lipstick, eye make-up, false eyelashes, face cream, face powder, films, travelling toothbrush, after-shave lotion, nail brush, small hairbrush, comb, small hand mirror, nail file or emery boards.

Stationers

Drawing pins, especially coloured ones, paper clips, Sellotape or scotch tape in various colours, rubber eraser, miniature stapler and staples, pencil sharpener, tiny notebook, rubber bands, photo corners, crayons, coloured pencils, ball point pens and felt pens (must be short enough to fit in the cracker), glue, string, self-adhesive labels in various colours, wrapping ribbon, penknife, pencils, book marker, watch strap, small purse, economy labels, sealing wax, small pack of cards.

Hardware stores and garden shops

Nails, screws, hooks, wall nails, picture hangers, curtain hooks, pocket screw driver set, small tins of paint and enamel, fabric and leather dye, duster, dish cloth, scourer, bottle opener, bottle brush, tacks, packets of seeds, flower bulbs, garden labels, garden ties.

Haberdashers and jewelry stores

Pins, needles, folding scissors, cotton, wool, press-studs and poppers, hooks and eyes, buttons, thread, safety pins, elastic, coloured ribbon, sew-on emblems, iron-on emblems, binding tape, shoe laces, zips, lace, pin-on artificial flowers and fruit, hair ornaments and slides, handkerchiefs, plastic rain hat, key ring, thimble, rings, brooches, ear-rings, beads and other jewelry, buckle, needle case, pincushion, head or neck scarf, scarf ring, tights, tape measure, charms.

Sweetshops and tobacconists

Loose sweets, either individually wrapped or packaged by you, lollipops, home-made sweets, miniature chocolate bars, chewing gum, chocolates, peppermints, stick of rock, sugar mice, etc, chocolate coins, chocolate sugar eggs, tubes and sticks of sweets, pipe cleaners, matches (the boxes can be decorated), small cigars, cigarettes, cigarette lighter.

Food stores

Foil-wrapped cheeses, stock cubes, garlic, peppers, herbs and spices in small bags, chocolate biscuits, small wrapped cakes, cake decorations, tubes of purée and sauces, packets of soup, party dips, pasta in small bags, picnic jams, nuts, teabags.

Toyshops and sports shops

Marbles, tops, toy soldiers, farm animals, zoo animals, cowboys and indians, spacemen, toy watches, divers-in-a-bottle, magnetic insects, dice, yoyos, miniature playing cards, 'Potty Putty', Plasticine, matchbox cars, toy aeroplanes and boats, fluffy animals, balls, puzzles, jokes and tricks, false moustaches, doll's clothing, balloons, doll's jewelry, toy money, jacks, badges, beads, toy cooking utensils and implements, torches, toy shopping items, gummed shapes, sticky paper, magnifying glass, cloth books and small paper-back books that can be rolled up, pipecleaner animals and people, bells, shells, china and wooden animals, miniature dolls, repair outfit for rubber tyres and footballs, golf tees, fishing line, weights, flies and hooks (these must be safely pre-packaged), golf balls, table tennis balls, draughts, travelling chess sets, darts (must be safely packaged), poker dice, tiddly winks, travelling dominoes, solitaire.

Kitchen shops

Pastry brush, small wooden spoon, small pastry cutters, teaspoons, wooden salt spoon, bouquets garnis, peelers and crushers which will fit in a cracker, meat needle, skewers, small butter moulds, wooden egg cups, jar labels, salt grinder, pepper grinder, sand egg-timer, pie frills, joint and cutlet frills, nut crackers, jam pot covers, oven thermometer, mustard pot.

Papers

The choice of papers for wrapping presents, making decorations or crackers is enormous — we have never had such a varied and exciting selection before and new ones keep appearing in the shops. They range from fine tissue paper in rainbow colours, through stretchy crepes, wrapping paper, flocked paper, foils, Cellophane, acetates and other plastic-based materials. You can get them fragile or strong, matt or shiny, patterned or plain, and of course by mixing them the permutations are limitless. According to their nature, they behave differently and some are much more appropriate than others for particular decorations. If you have difficulty in getting any of the papers mentioned here in your local stores, write to one of the addresses given on page 100 for a complete range and price list.

Crackers are essentially made to be pulled apart and the thinner papers are usually the most suitable for the basic form, reserving the heavier-textured, plastic and foil papers for surface decoration. It is not impossible to use the stronger papers, but they should be perforated to prevent a rather embarrassing tug-of-war at the table.

Let us start with the lightest (and cheapest): tissue paper is ideal for crackers and interesting effects and patterns can be achieved by mixing and matching the multitude of colours.

fig. 35

Single crepe is the paper most commonly seen on bought crackers, and is very suitable. Foil crepe and duplex crepe both consist of a double layer of paper and their thick crinkly texture makes a richer, more lavish cracker, whether used for the whole or only a part. The unusual 'glass' crepe is a crinkled and extremely tough Cellophane, and should be reserved for frills. Because the peculiar character of crepe paper allows it to be shaped and moulded between the fingertips, it is also particularly suitable for making flowers, and examples of these are described in Chapter 9.

Metallic papers play an important part in all sorts of festive and special-occasion decorations. There are some beautiful colours in plain paper-backed foil, and whether used in

figs. 36-39

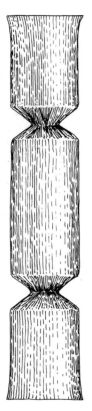

figs. 40-44

crackers, flowers, or other table decorations, you should try to use it where its special reflective quality can be emphasized by lights and candles. Alternatively, foils can be used as the background for lace, braid, the delicate Japanese lacy paper and other papers with cut-out patterns. As well as the paper-back foils, there are relief printed foils and foil acetates, which are equally attractive, but all of them are too stiff to be used other than as dramatic additions. Even the very thin metallized polyester, Melinex, is generally too strong, whether perforated or not, for the basic cracker.

Flocked paper is another 'heavy-weight', to be reserved for decoration, but its velvety surface makes it a very attractive and rich contrast to the shiny papers, or to frills of net and crepe.

43

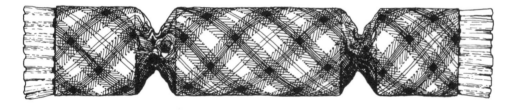

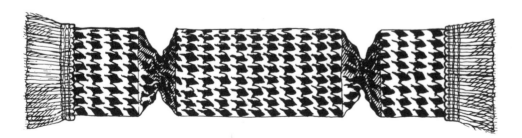

You are probably already familiar with the wide choice of patterned wrapping paper — stripes, spots, abstract designs, flowers, pictures, words, etc. Do not forget the pretty paper you can buy for lining shelves and drawers, and the odds and ends of wall paper you may have in a cupboard. Crackers can always be decorated with additions of small pieces of paper, but you must remember to choose complementary colours and patterns. Some basic papers invite a particular decoration, such as the woollen braid edging on the 'tweed' paper (page 44). Others, such as the fur pattern (page 45) and the snakeskin (page 44) are perfect as they are and would be spoilt by further decoration. Stripes — straight, diagonal or zig-zag — are probably amongst the most successful patterns, because of their simplicity and crispness.

If you are careful when cutting your papers you will find that a relatively small amount will go a long way. Here are a few statistics showing what you can expect to make from your paper.

One roll of single crepe (measuring 20 x 102 inches or 51 x 259 cm) makes sixteen crackers and the piece left over will make eight more if it is cut in half and the two half-width strips stuck together. Thus you can make two dozen crackers from one roll, and the economics of making your own crackers begin to look interesting.

One yard (91 cm) of foil crepe (30 inches or 76 cm wide) will make ten crackers, and a roll (19 x 99 inches or 48 x 250 cm) will make sixteen crackers.

One sheet of plain or patterned wrapping paper (29½ x 20½ inches or 75 x 52 cm) makes six crackers, although if you want to have folded-in ends you will only get three out of a sheet.

A sheet of tissue paper (30 x 20½ inches or 76 x 52 cm) will make six crackers, and this is probably the most economical material of all.

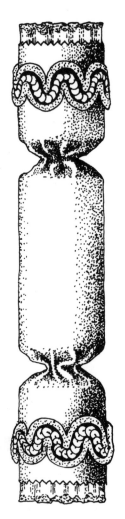

6 Frills and Decorations

In this chapter I am describing the frills and decorations which can be added to the basic cracker without disguising or transforming it.

At two different stages during cracker-making the decorations can be added. In the main, the banded decorations are added to the flat papers before the crackers are assembled — a much neater method than if they are added to the completed cracker, as the rolling motion in assembly will shape the band. Any object like a badge or a flower placed on the surface will of course be attached when the basic shape is complete, as indeed are frills, which would be squashed if they were added before rolling.

A great many materials are suitable for banded decorations, from ribbon and cord to lace, braid (fig. 52) and tinsel (Plate 3) and by assembling papers of more than one kind you can produce most interesting results. The strips of paper which remain after the cracker papers have been cut from a roll or sheet can be put to good use either as bands or, if it is crepe paper, as frills. From a standard roll of crepe paper the strip which remains when crackers have been made is exactly the required width for frills and it is perhaps worth mentioning here that, as the waste strip is also exactly half the width of a full-size cracker, two waste strips can be joined, with a band concealing the join, to make complete crackers. I have seen a

figs. 52-56
Banded decorations

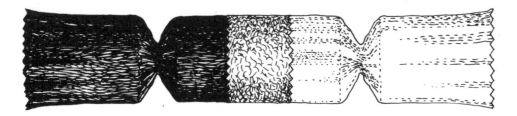

fig. 57

fig. 58

most striking box of crackers made in this way with black and white papers joined with a gold band (fig. 57).

The material you use for making bands need not be cut in plain strips. Sometimes the pattern on the paper will suggest a wavy design, as shown in fig. 56.

One material which is particularly well suited for bands is perforated ribbon which is really the waste material from making sequins. When applied to a plain cracker as a broad band or in strips, this very simple decoration can be most effective (fig. 58). Luckily, the ribbon comes in a width which matches the central part of the cracker, and if the basic cracker is made of transparent cellulose film the gift parcel inside the cracker can be seen through the holes in the sequin ribbon. Such a device would have appealed to the Victorians!

You may wish to paint or draw a pattern of your own design on a plain paper. The scope for design is wide, from spots and stripes to overall effects created by masking and spraying paints.

I would suggest that metallic paints are preferable for Christmas and they contrast well with crepe paper.

Glitter dust can be added, and if it is applied as soon as you have sprayed with paint it will be held on by the damp paint. Beware of using too much glitter; it has its own special texture which is enhanced when used sparingly (fig. 62). The best place to use glitter is on the edges of frills, where the varying angles will mean that some is sure to catch the light.

Frilly Crackers

The basic cracker will need strength if frills are to be added to the two ends. An additional piece of stiffening card like that used in the centre is required at each end, and this, cut to lie on the cracker plan between the end of the cracker and the nearest former line at each end, can be glued to the lining paper before the cracker is made, or rolled later, pushed into the ends and stapled there for strength and permanence. This extra strength is important for without it the cracker would collapse when the frills are added.

Of all forms of decoration it is the frills which most readily transform the cylinder into an exotic, extravagant shape. Net, lace, Melinex or tissue as well as crepe paper can all be used to create billowing piles of frills. The trouble is that good design can be lost unless you are careful in your choice of colours and materials. If, for example, you choose to use three colours for the frills make sure that one of them is the same colour as the basic cracker. The cracker in fig. 59 has a zig-zag piece of paper in the centre to match the frills at the ends. If you make frills from the same material as is used for the basic cracker, it can look a little ordinary, and it is improved by adding tinsel or glitter or even coloured cellulose tape (fig. 64). This is an excellent material which transforms the silhouette of the frills when added to the stretched edge of crepe paper.

Frilly crackers made largely of foil crepe can be quite exotic, as in fig. 67, where the three layers of frills are shaped to

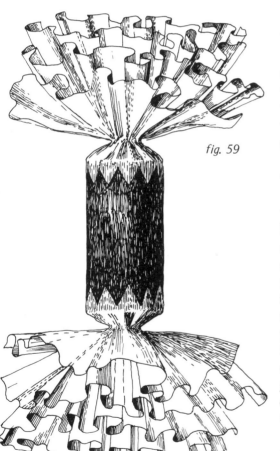

fig. 59

49

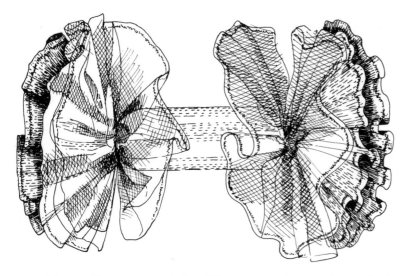

fig. 60

resemble a Canterbury bell. Glass crepe is another of the unusual crepe papers which is extremely effective for making transparent puffs at either end (fig. 65).

A more traditional material is net, which is not too successful when used on its own unless the frills are extremely full and plentiful. If it is used as an overskirt to a matching crepe paper, however, the result is rewarding (fig. 60). There is no need to keep the edges of frills straight. Crepe paper can be given a wavy edge, but the outline will be more clearly seen if the edges are lined with glitter (fig. 62). This design has been used by cracker manufacturers since 1900.

A material like Melinex can be cut into fine fringes with confidence, for it does not tear easily, and remains springy even when shapes have been cut out of it. Fig. 61 shows how severe

fig. 61

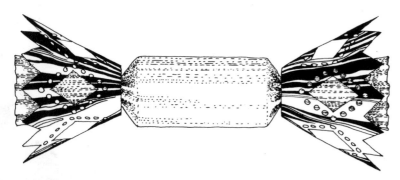

Melinex outlines can be softened by cutting patterns into the material.

Cracker Frills

In addition to the materials noted below for each type of frill you will need the materials for making a crepe paper cracker.

Glitter-edged Frills

Materials Crepe paper, glitter, foil crepe, glue.

Cut a piece of crepe paper 9 x 7 inches (23 x 18 cm) and frill the ends. Cut four small strips 7 x 4 inches (18 x 10 cm) of matching crepe, frill the edges and fold one so that the lower part of the fold projects ¼ inch (0.5 cm) beyond the upper edge. Then place this folded piece on top of a second strip so that the frill of the strip projects ¼ inch (0.5 cm) beyond the folded piece (fig. 63a). Now fold up the bottom part of the strip and the result will be four rows of frills spaced at ¼ inch intervals. Put a line of glue near the fold (fig. b) and lay the large piece of crepe paper on top of the four frills as in fig. c, continuing to keep them evenly spaced. Make frills out of the other two strips of paper for the opposite end, and attach them to the large sheet in the same way. Put a line of glue along the edges of all the frills and press them into a tray of glitter. Then assemble the cracker in the normal way. Finally, attach the centre band of foil crepe 7 x 3 inches (18 x 7.5 cm).

fig. 62

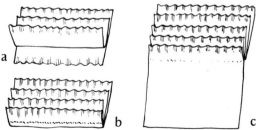

fig. 63

Tape-edged Frills

Materials Crepe paper, coloured cellulose tape, binding wire.

Make a basic cracker of crepe paper in the normal way, using
the off-cut from the roll to make the frill. (This piece should
measure 18 x 8¼ inches or 45.5 x 21 cm.) Fold it so that one
edge of the fold projects about 1 inch (2.5 cm) beyond the

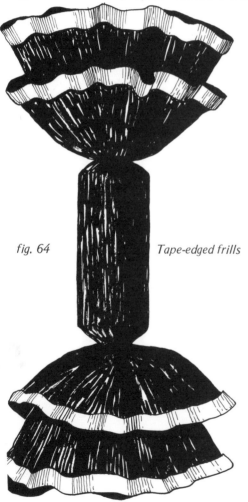

fig. 64   Tape-edged frills

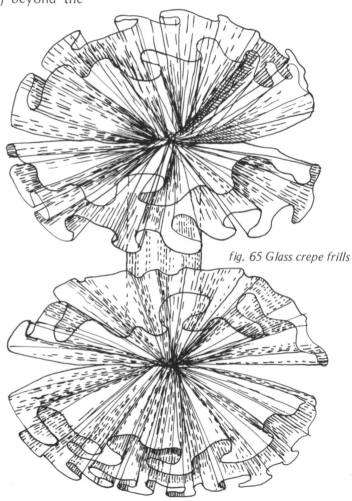

fig. 65 Glass crepe frills

other. Frill these two edges and stick a strip of tape along both of the frills. Thread binding wire through the fold and gather the paper until the gathered edge measures about 2 inches (5 cm). Now attach the frills to the cracker by placing them around the choke and twisting the ends of the wire together. Make a second frill and attach in the same way to the other choke.

Glass Crepe Frills

Materials Glass crepe paper, binding wire.

Make a cracker of crepe paper in the usual way. Cut four pieces of glass crepe measuring 25½ x 7½ inches (65 x 19 cm) and fold each exactly in half lengthways. Arrange two of the folded pieces together and thread a binding wire through the fold. Gather all the frills and attach to the cracker in the way described for the tape-edged frills. The strong glass crepe will spring open partly to cover the central area of the cracker.

A similar cracker can be made with frills of different materials, for example, one frill of net and one of crepe at each end (see fig. 60). In this case each frill must be attached separately.

Foil Frills

Materials Melinex (or other foil or acetate film), binding wire.

Make a cracker of crepe paper in the normal way, but cover the central section with the same foil as you will use for the frills. Cut two pieces of thin Melinex 21½ x 4¾ inches (54 x 12 cm). Fold each piece lengthways so that one edge projects about 1½ inches (4 cm) beyond the other. Thread binding wire through the fold, gather and attach the frills as described for the cracker with tape-edged frills. The springy Melinex will open out towards the centre.

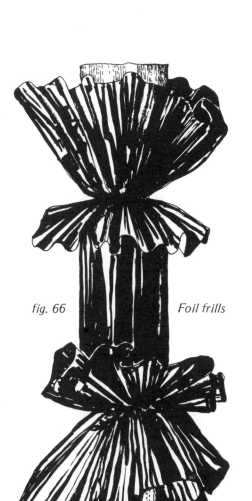

fig. 66   Foil frills

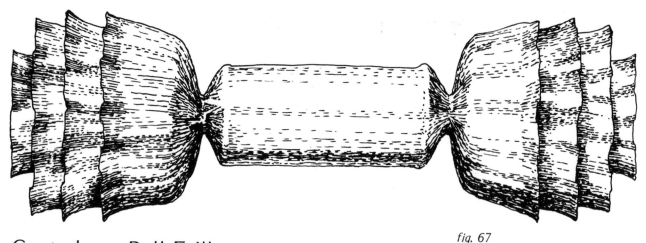

fig. 67

Canterbury Bell Frills

Materials Foil crepe, glue, binding wire.

Because of the cost of foil crepe, this is the most extravagant cracker in the whole book. First make a basic cracker out of crepe paper, and cover the central section and the two chokes with a piece of foil crepe 6 x 6 inches (15 x 15 cm). Cut two strips of foil crepe 6¾ x 1½ inches (17 x 4 cm), fold them in half lengthways and glue them to the ends of the cracker so that the crepe paper is hidden (fig. 68a). Then frill the triple-thickness ends of the cracker. Cut three pieces of foil crepe 11¾ x 4 inches (30 x 10 cm), 11¾ x 3½ inches (30 x 9 cm) and 11¾ x 3 inches (30 x 7.5 cm). Frill along one side of each of these pieces, put glue along the unfrilled side and stick them together as shown in fig. **b**. Make a ½ inch (1 cm) fold at the glued edge, enclosing a piece of binding wire in the fold (fig. **c**). Gather and attach this triple frill as described for the tape-edged frills. Make frills for the other end and attach them in the same way.

   Foil crepe is very strong. This complicated construction is necessary if the cracker is to come to pieces at the required time.

fig. 68

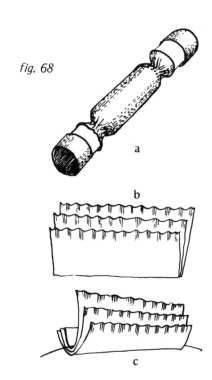

a

b

c

54

Petal Frills

Materials Crepe paper, glitter, binding wire and glue.

Make a cracker of crepe paper in the normal way. Cut four pieces of matching crepe paper 7 x 1½ inches (18 x 4 cm) and cut both long edges into petal shapes as in fig. 69. Fold the pieces to make two sets of frills as described for the glitter-edged frills (page 51). Put a line of glue along the edges of the petals and press them into a tray of glitter. Gather and attach the frills with binding wire as described for the tape-edged frills.

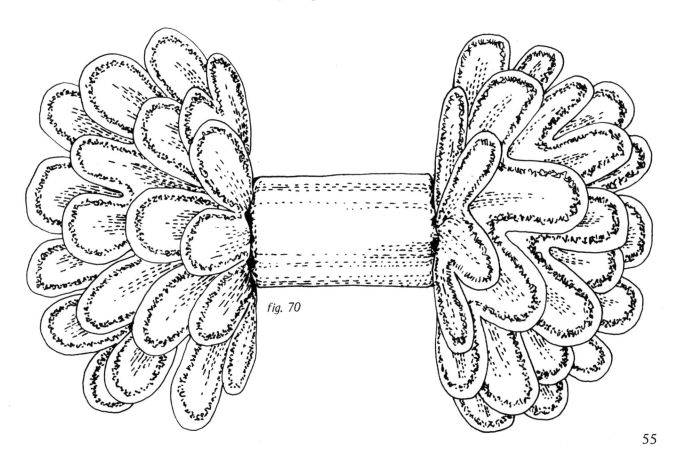

fig. 69

fig. 70

Central Motifs

Originally the centres of crackers were adorned with small pictures or gummed scraps which gave a clue as to their contents. The centre decoration can be very elaborate, with artificial flowers and buds or real toys attached to the middle of the cracker on the outside. Often such decorations can be too heavy for the supporting cracker. It is important that the crackers should lie easily on the table and not be rolling over all the time because their decoration is too ornate or weighty. Miniature flower decorations, being light, are very suitable for decorating the centre part. An average of 1 inch (2.5 cm) in total diameter is a good guide to follow as a suitable size for miniature flowers. The whole of Chapter 9 is concerned with making flowers, and some of the flowers described there are ideal for decorating the centre of crackers. Particularly suitable are the Little Bells and Roses, described on pages 87 and 86. Single flowers can be surrounded by leaves, and tied together as a spray with a strip of ribbon before being glued to the front of the cracker.

Many natural materials such as fir cones, dried grasses and everlasting flowers can be used to make up flower sprays, or used as they are in the centre of the cracker. Plain and patterned feathers can also be useful, and they contrast well in texture with ribbon. White turkey neck feathers are good (fig. 73); alternatively, patterned pheasant feathers can be used for flowers or for banded decorations. Other materials you might try include seeds and shells, many of which can make stunning designs if you have plenty of patience (fig. 74).

Ribbon is about the most versatile material of all for cracker decoration. The self-adhesive decorative parcel ribbon, for example, is particularly easy to use, and can be made into flowers, loops and rings (fig. 75) as well as used in straightforward bands. A rather tricky but extremely attractive little rose can be made with ribbon, showing off the shiny surface of the self-adhesive ribbon to advantage. There is a velvet-textured

figs. 71-75

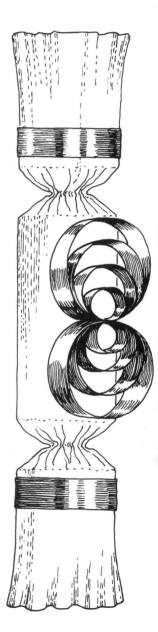

florist's ribbon (fig. 76) with a satinized edge which lends itself well to making this flower, and if you use such material in the centre of the cracker it is a good idea to use it again at the cracker's ends to make bands.

You will note that I have stressed the importance of contrast in creating decorations, but remember, too, that an attractive material used in making the basic cracker can sometimes be effective if used for the decorations as well, as shown in fig. 77.

The Butterfly

Materials Melinex, or another of the acetate films, binding wire, four beads, glue, in addition to the usual cracker-making materials.

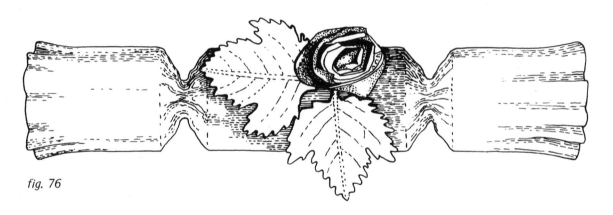

fig. 76

fig. 77

Cut a square of Melinex and fold it in half. Cut the half-butterfly shape as in fig. 79 and open out. To make the body cut a piece of binding wire 4¾ inches (12 cm) long, fold it in half and thread on the four beads. Bend up the loop to prevent the beads falling off and curl the ends of the wire to make the antennae (fig. 80). Glue the body into the fold of the wings and then glue the butterfly on to the cracker.

A simpler butterfly can be made by cutting the shape out of Melinex and then making a cut down the front edge of the larger wings while they are still folded together, as in fig. 81. When you open out the butterfly these strips of Melinex will spring up to form the antennae.

fig. 78

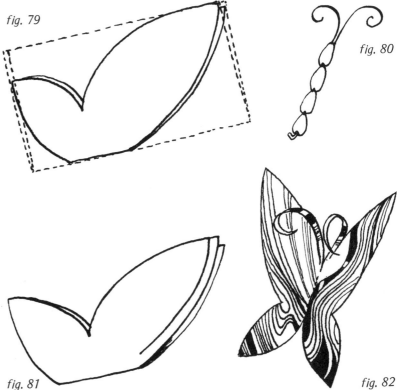

fig. 79

fig. 80

fig. 81

fig. 82

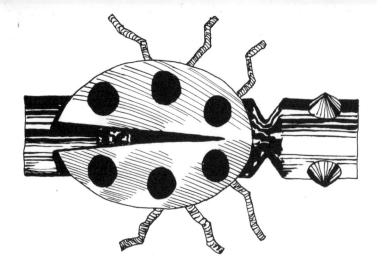

figs. 83-85 Creepy-crawly crackers

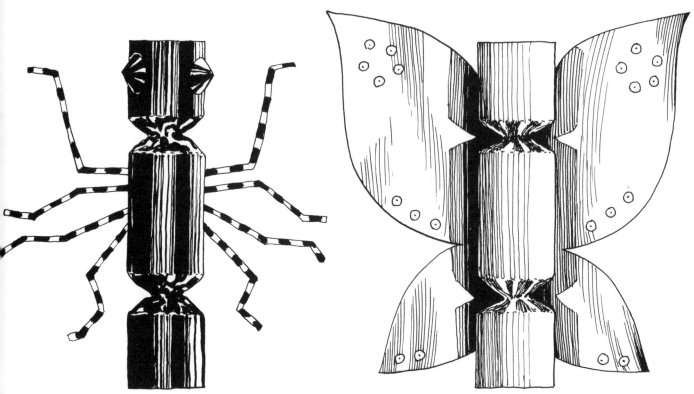

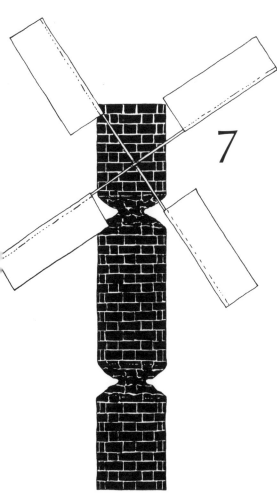

fig. 86 The Windmill cracker. To make it stand upright you have to weight the base.

7 Crackers for Children

Children often enjoy tearing things to bits, but they do not appreciate all the effort that goes into making crackers. Try, therefore, to keep designs for children simple and striking. If you are making crackers for a children's party, you may well have a child helper, and so avoid difficult designs which can look disappointing if they are not neatly put together.

The conventional shape of crackers makes it natural for them to lie flat rather than to stand, and crackers designed to stand on their own are unexpected and very striking. Their proportions have to be changed to give them a broad or weighty base, and as soon as this is done there is a flood of new ideas for recognizable forms that will be a delight to a child. A silver moon rocket, for example, can be made to stand by adding a skirt of acetate foil. Printed brick paper can be used for the 'body' of a windmill or a lighthouse, and the details can be added at the top. Mail boxes can be made out of bright red paper, or each cracker, made out of grey brick paper, can represent the turret of a castle, with a castellated top and a folded paper 'wall' joining the places at the table. If a castle is used as a table centre decoration, the crackers can be made to look like sentries or guardsmen.

If you start with the basic shape of the cylinder there are several horizontal subjects which have great appeal for children. By the addition of some cardboard wheels an engine cracker suitably decorated can pull a whole train of cracker wagons behind it down the centre of a long table. A steam engine cracker is described on page 66.

If not wheels, but legs, are added then a whole menagerie of animals is possible. Pipe cleaner legs and cardboard wings instantly transform chubby crackers into spiders, ladybirds or butterflies, as shown on page 60. The paper hedgehog wrapped with fringes of black crepe paper (fig. 96) is rather time-consuming, but a standard cracker covered with a parted fringe of yellow rug wool and a cardboard face glued to one end quickly becomes a familiar television character.

For children, the proportions of the basic cracker can be shortened by simply folding the ends of the papers in by 2 inches (5 cm) at each end or by making a chubby cracker, as described below. The result is easier for small children to handle, and takes up less space on a crowded table, and it is also a more stable shape if the crackers are to be displayed vertically. Such short crackers look well as funnels in simple cardboard ships which sail down the party table in fleets.

fig. 87 A ship with cracker funnels

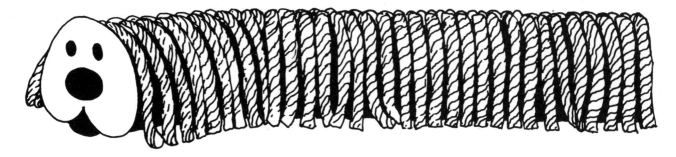

fig. 88 An animal cracker

fig. 89 Chubby crackers

When making crackers for children's parties, time is often at a premium and ready-made 'funny-face' badges or plastic stickers used as central decorations save time and give much pleasure, for the badges can be unpinned and worn. Badges with different and distinct designs, incidentally, help you to identify and distribute crackers which are more suitable for girls than for boys, and vice versa. Making crackers for children is very rewarding and a few unusual ideas are described fully on the pages that follow. One thing is certain, however, children's crackers will not last long, so do not use extravagant papers — tissue paper is the best of all: it is cheap and easily broken open.

Chubby Cracker

Materials Tissue paper, lining paper, stiffener card, snap, gift and glue.

Cut a piece of tissue paper 12½ x 6 inches (32 x 15 cm) and cut a piece of stiffener card 6 x 2½ inches (15 x 6.5 cm). Assemble the cracker by placing the piece of lining paper on top of the tissue paper and fold the ends of the tissue paper in 2 inches (5 cm) at each end. Place the stiffener card in the centre in the usual way. You will find that the parts of your cracker do not line up with the marks on the cracker plan, as it has shorter sections. Before making the first choke, align the edge of the stiffener card with former line **c**, and place the other end of the stiffener card on former line **b** before making the second choke.

63

Cracker Castle

Materials Several sheets of 'stone-wall' doll's house paper, a piece of card, 8 stiffener cards, 8 snaps, 8 mottoes, gifts and glue.

Cut eight pieces of paper 12 x 6 inches (30.5 x 15 cm) with the stone course running across them, and make up eight crackers. Then cut battlements out of one end of each cracker. Cut eight pieces of card 7 x 3¼ inches (18 x 8 cm) and cover them on both sides with stone-wall paper; then cut battlements along the top of each one. Place two of these walls on edge, and join them by glueing a 'hinge' of stone-wall paper measuring about 2¾ x 1¼ inches (7 x 3 cm) on the inside of the corner. Repeat this with the other seven corners, and you will have a 'curtain wall' of cardboard that will stand up. Now apply a little glue to each corner and attach the crackers so that they stand like towers.

You may want to put a large tower inside your castle wall, as shown in the illustration. You can build this in the same way as the outer wall, and add cracker towers at different heights up its walls.

The castle shown opposite has enough crackers for a party with more than twenty children.

Steam Engine Cracker

Materials Coloured card, black shiny paper, metallic cellulose tape, stiffening card, snap, motto, gifts and glue.

Cut the piece of black shiny paper 12½ x 6 inches (32 x 15 cm) and make up a chubby cracker (see page 63). Put two bands of cellulose tape around the centre. Cut a piece of card 10½ x 2¾ inches (27 x 7 cm), make two score marks 2 inches (5 cm) apart

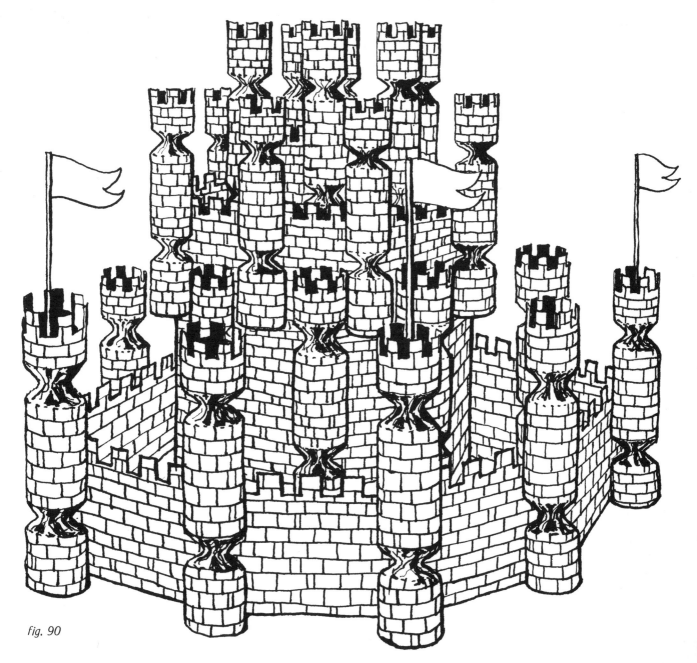

fig. 90

65

as shown in fig. 91a, and cut a hole out of each side. Place the folded card over one end of the cracker to form the cab. Cut four large disks and two small ones out of thick card and stick them in place to put the engine 'on wheels' and to raise the cracker off the table. Another piece of card can be cut and glued to the front of the cab if you wish, as shown in fig. 91b. Make a tube out of black shiny paper to form the funnel and glue this to one end of the cracker as shown in the drawing.

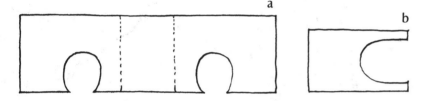

fig. 91

fig. 92 The engine cracker's wagons can be individual crackers with wheels or a cardboard trailer filled with crackers.

Plate 3 Foil crackers decorated with tinsel.

Moon Rocket

Materials Silver wrapping paper, metallic cellulose tape, Melinex, stiffener card, snap, motto, gifts and glue.

Cut a piece of silver wrapping paper 12½ x 6 inches (32 x 15 cm) and assemble a cracker in the normal way. To make the nose of the rocket cut a piece of Melinex 4 inches (10 cm) in diameter as shown for the hedgehog (p. 71) and shape it into a cone. Glue this on the top of the cracker. For the skirt of the rocket use Melinex again, but this time cut a fan-shaped piece with a radius of 4 inches (10 cm) in the shape shown in fig. 94 and staple this into a funnel shape on the end of the cracker. Finally put a band of metallic sellotape on to the centre of the cracker to complete the rocket. The rocket can stand on the table pointing upwards, ready for take-off.

Maypole

Materials A cardboard tube (a long roll of kitchen foil will have one of suitable size in its centre), tissue paper of more than one shade, ribbon of two colours, lining paper, cardboard cake stand, pin holder, stiffener cards, snaps, mottoes, gifts and glue.

Make one cracker for each person. Cut the cracker papers to 12½ x 6 inches (32 x 15 cm) so that the result will be chubby-size crackers. Take both colours of ribbon and make a bow to fix at the top of the cardboard tube. Stand the pin holder in the centre of the cake stand, cover both with tissue paper and then stand the cardboard tube in the centre. Cut a piece of ribbon for each cracker approximately 20 inches (50 cm) long and glue these to the inside of the top of the tube, arranging the colours alternately. Plait the ribbons around the maypole to about half way down and secure with glue where they touch the pole.

Plate 4 A gold and copper arrangement containing foil crepe roses (p. 86-7), melinex flowers (p. 88), double foil crepe bells and frilly poppies with tinsel centres (p. 87).

fig. 93

fig. 94

Then take the remainder of each ribbon out to a cracker and staple the end of the ribbon into the end of the cracker. Arrange the crackers to stand on end around the maypole. You may have difficulty in keeping them upright if the crackers are not weighted near their base, and an alternative method is to staple them firmly round the side of the cake stand.

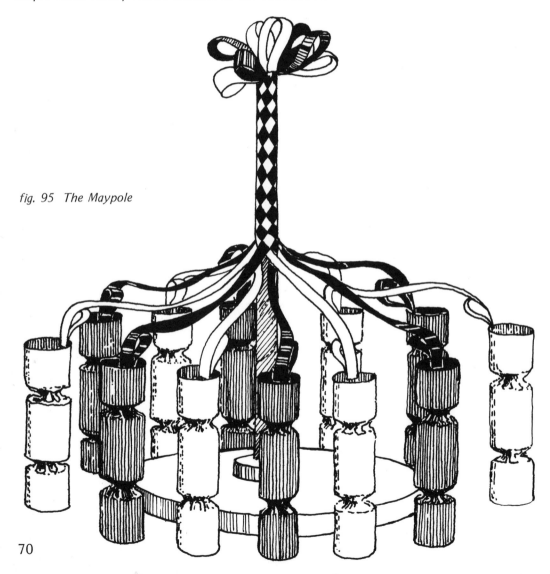

fig. 95 The Maypole

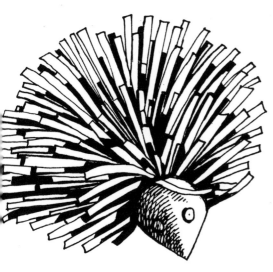

fig. 96

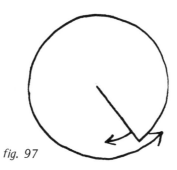

fig. 97

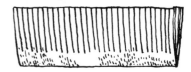

fig. 98

Hedgehog

Materials Black shiny paper, crepe paper, lining paper, stiffener card, snap, binding wire, gift and glue.

Make a chubby cracker (see page 63) of black crepe paper. Next cut a circle of black shiny paper 4 inches (10 cm) in diameter. Slit this to the centre and fold it into a cone shape as in fig. 97, stapling the overlapping sides together. Apply glue to the inside of the cone and place it over one end of the cracker, forcing the soft ends of the black crepe as far as possible into the cone. Glue on two sequins for eyes as shown in the drawing.

Cut four strips of black crepe paper 12 x 8 inches (30 x 20 cm). Place the strips together and fold over lengthways. From the open end make parallel cuts 3 inches (7.5 cm) into the paper so that it looks like a comb (fig. 98). Next thread a piece of binding wire through, close to the fold, and gather the paper together, so that it frills out. Place this frill around the choke of the cracker nearest to the hedgehog's head and secure by twisting the binding wire together on the underside. With four more pieces of black crepe repeat the process and tie a second ruff of paper 'prickles' around the choke near to the tail end. The prickles will fall into an attractive shape unaided, but you can round them off with scissors if you wish.

8   Very Special Crackers

The first cracker-makers, the Victorians, went to endless lengths to produce a great variety of very special crackers. Some of their inventive designs are still popular today, for example, a favourite which has stayed with us is the one giant cracker filled with lots of parcels which tumble everywhere when the monster is pulled by all guests together.

There are many occasions when it seems a shame to pull and destroy the crackers you have made, especially when it comes to the rather macabre business of tearing to pieces a cracker which represents a person. In such cases the structure can be modified so that the contents can be removed without destroying the outer wrapping. Some early crackers have small doors fitted into their sides so that the gift can be taken out like a treasure from a safe. Such devices are useful if you make 'people crackers', as shown and described on pages 75-8. A large frill at one end makes the skirt, leaving only paper arms, face and a hat to be made at the other. You can make characters like gipsies, Spanish dancers and crinolined ladies, and even clowns and soldiers with outsize feet as a means of standing them up.

Flower Crackers

Petals or frills can turn the end of a cracker into a bloom, and in the case of a daffodil the trumpet is already made in the basic

fig. 99

shape. Other flowers are possible, too, and the snap can be incorporated in the design as one of the stamens. A basket of flower crackers as shown in fig. 99 makes a decorative centre piece at a summer party.

Daffodil Cracker

Materials Green crepe paper, orange crepe paper, white duplex crepe, lining paper, stiffener card, binding wire, snap, motto, gift and glue.

Cut a piece of green crepe paper 9 x 6¾ inches (23 x 17 cm) and a piece of orange crepe paper 6¾ x 4 inches (17 x 10 cm). Lay the green piece on your cracker plan with one side on the end line. The other end should just cross the string crease line at the other end. Run a line of glue along this end. Now lay down the orange piece so that it completes the full length of the basic cracker, sticking it to the green crepe with the glue. Assemble the cracker in the normal way, and then make six petals with the duplex crepe, 5 x 3¼ inches (13 x 8 cm) cutting them according to fig. 116a. Fold ¾ inch (2 cm) back at the base of each petal and arrange the petals side by side on a binding wire by threading it through the folds, glueing the fold to the petal if necessary. Gather the petals until the gathered edge measures about 2 inches (5 cm). Now fix the crepe petals around the orange trumpet at one end by placing them round the choke and twisting the ends of the wire together, to make a daffodil like those shown in fig. 99. To make a neat arrangement, it may be necessary to make the petals overlap, and this should be done when they are finally in place on the cracker.

Lady Cracker

Materials Crepe paper in two colours, plus pink for the face, lining paper, two stiffener cards, glitter, binding wire, snap, motto, gift and glue.

Choose the paper you require for the body and make up a basic cracker but do not frill the ends. Cut the remaining stiffener card in half lengthways, apply glue to both pieces and stick them inside the ends of the cracker (fig. 101a). Cut a piece of crepe 20 x 11¾ inches (50 x 30 cm) for the underskirt, and fold it in half lengthways as in fig. b (notice the direction of the grain). Run a line of glue along both the long sides and dip them in glitter (fig. c). Now apply glue to the centre, which will be at the waistline on the cracker. Thread binding wire inside the fold, gather it together and fix it to the waist, twisting the ends of the wire together (fig. d). If the skirt does not comfortably overlap, a little glue can be added to fix the two sides together. Frill the two glittered edges of the skirt, separating the layers.

fig. 100

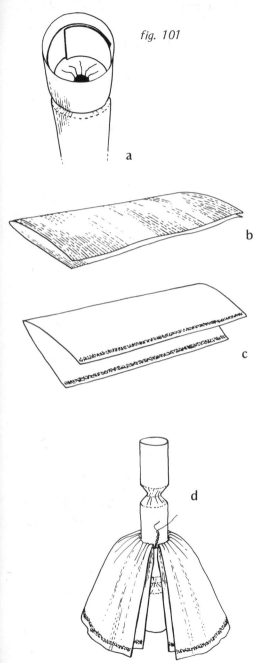

fig. 101

a

b

c

d

Use the contrasting crepe paper for an overskirt. Cut a piece 20 x 6½ inches (50 x 16 cm) and fold one of the long sides over for about 1 inch (2.5 cm), if necessary securing the fold with a little glue. Thread binding wire through this fold and twist the crepe paper round the waist on top of the underskirt. Repeat this procedure with another layer, this time measuring 27½ x 11¾ inches (70 x 30 cm).

Cut a piece of stiffening card 5 x 2½ inches (13 x 6 cm) to make the top of the dress and cover it with a piece of contrasting crepe paper 6½ x 3½ inches (16 x 9 cm). Leave one end of the crepe projecting, as shown in fig. 102a. Now cut a door out of the back of the cracker (fig. b) and glue the piece of card around the body of the cracker as shown in fig. c, sticking the projecting crepe flap down with glue to close the door.

To make the arms, cut a piece of crepe paper 7 x 1½ inches (18 x 4 cm) and fold it lengthways into three layers (fig. d). Secure the folds with a little glue. Note the direction of the grain shown in the figure. Fold the centre diagonally to form the hands and then diagonally again to form the elbows, as shown in fig. e. Make a fan with a small piece of crepe paper 2½ x 1¼ inches (6 x 3 cm) and glue it on the inside of the hands (fig. f). Glue the arms on at the shoulders (fig. g).

Cut a piece of pink crepe paper 3¼ inches (8 cm) wide and draw a face on it as in fig. h. Then apply a little glue to the inside and stick the face in position. To make the hat, cut two pieces of crepe paper 3½ x 4½ inches (9 x 11 cm) and stick them back to back. Cut them into an oval shape and make star-shaped cuts in the centre as in fig. i. Now cut another piece 3½ x ¾ inches (9 x 2 cm) and make short cuts along it (fig. j). Push up the point of the star as in fig. k and fix on the second piece as in fig. l. Make a further piece and stick this to the crown of the hat (fig. m). To make the feather cut two pieces of crepe paper 2¾ x 2 inches (7 x 5 mm) as in fig. n. Glue them together up the centre, sandwiching a piece of binding wire between them and make cuts all along both

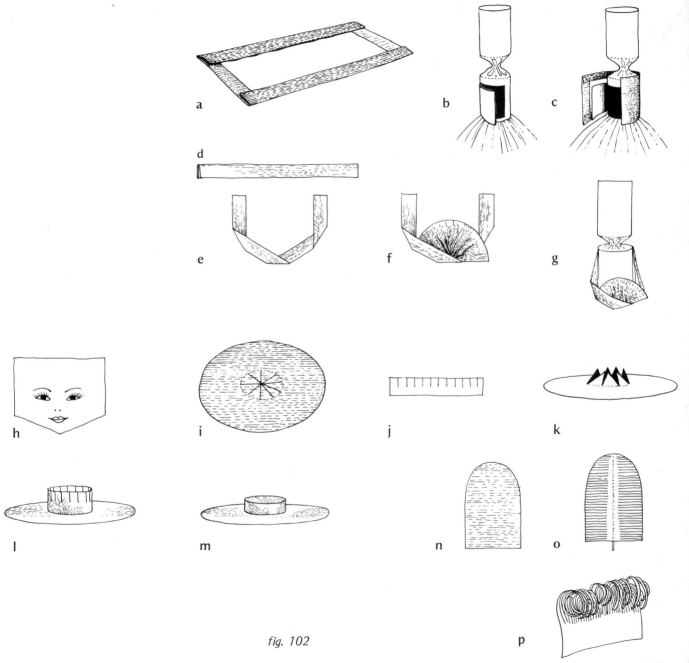

fig. 102

77

sides (fig. **o**). Curl this double piece over a scissor blade so that the whole feather curves and then stick it on to the hat. Before you make the hair, fold over the soft crepe at the top of the cracker and secure with a little glue if necessary. The hair is built up with several layers of strips which are cut like a comb and curled over a scissor blade (fig. **p**). These strips are approximately 3½ x 3½ inches (9 x 9 cm) but the size and number will of course vary according to the hairstyle you choose. Start at the neck and add layers of hair until the head is covered. You will need to add a strip facing forwards to frame the face (fig. 103) before glueing on the hat.

The character of your people can vary enormously, and you can dress and design them to suit your party. The picture on page 72 shows several different kinds.

fig. 103

Geometric Crackers

The accepted shape for crackers is a cylinder, but equally effective results can be achieved by using square, triangular, or in fact any geometrical straight-sided shapes. On the whole the simpler the shape the better, especially for the standard size cracker. Triangular and square crackers lie satisfactorily on the table and fit snugly in a box.

fig. 105

Triangular Crackers

Materials Crepe paper, foil card, snap, motto and gift.

Cut the crepe paper 11 x 5½ inches (28 x 14 cm). Cut three pieces of foil card, one 5½ x 3½ inches (14 x 9 cm) and the

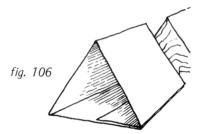

fig. 106

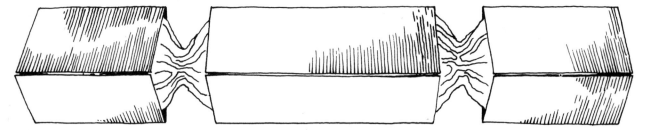

fig. 104

fig. 107 Cage Cracker

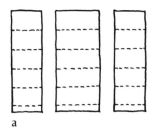

a

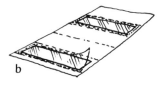

b

c

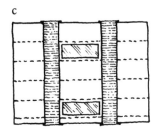

fig. 108

other two 5½ x 2½ inches (14 x 6 cm). Place the pieces as if ready for assembly, with the foil side uppermost. Score the surfaces in three places down the length of all the pieces, 1½ inches (4 cm) apart, as shown in fig. 105, leaving a strip ¾ inch (2 cm) wide at the right side. Apply glue to the under-surface of the cards and place them on the crepe paper. Make sure that the cards at each end are level with the ends of the crepe.

Now apply glue along the ¾ inch (2 cm) strip at the side of the card and fold it up into a triangular shape as shown in fig. 106. When it is firmly glued, make the cracker chokes in the normal way, but remember that there is no former in the construction to give it strength in making, and so take care that the snap and the gift do not fall out.

Square section crackers are made by making four score lines instead of three.

Cage Crackers

Materials Crepe paper, card, clear cellulose film, lining paper, stiffener card, motto, glue and gift.

Cut three pieces of card one 6½ x 3½ inches (16 x 9 cm) and two 6½ x 2½ inches (16 x 6 cm) according to fig. 108a and score along the lines. Make the two small windows by cutting out rectangular shapes and lining them with clear cellulose film (fig. b). Lay the three pieces of card in position on the cracker plan and glue strips of matching crepe paper in position to fill the gaps (fig. c). Crease the cardboard parts along the scored lines and glue the joints firmly together. Insert the gift and complete the cracker by making the chokes in the usual way.

fig. 109

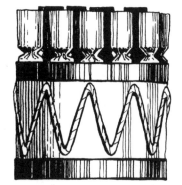

fig.
110

Special Presentation

Even simple crackers can become part of an elaborate display. At your party, crackers look their most spectacular if they are carefully arranged together rather than laid around the table with the place settings. A bundle of crackers tied with yards of ribbon (fig. 114) in the centre of the table is one of the simplest yet most attractive ways of presenting them. Otherwise a strip of decorated card can be made into a ring in which to stand the crackers up on end. The ring can vary from a crown complete with sparking 'jewels' and cotton wool 'fur' to a drum with zig-zag line of string around it. With the use of card containers, the crackers will become elements in a single design. A fan of crackers, for example, as shown in fig. 109 is attractive whilst saving space at the same time. To make this, all you have to do is to take a circular piece of card, crease it twice near the centre, sew the crackers to the base and hold the two sides of the fan together with a small piece of card. In this design the decoration on the crackers is repeated on the fan itself.

fig.
111

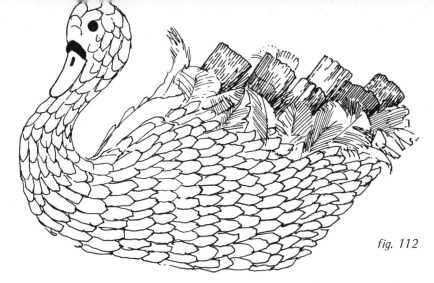

fig. 112

A sophisticated version of the children's fleet of ships described in the last chapter is shown in fig. 113 — crackers carried in a simple cardboard gondola. An equally graceful container can be made to resemble a swan (fig. 112) and a touch of reality is achieved by adding white feathers to the tops of all the crackers. All these card containers have the advantage of folding flat and thus can be stored away for future years.

fig. 113

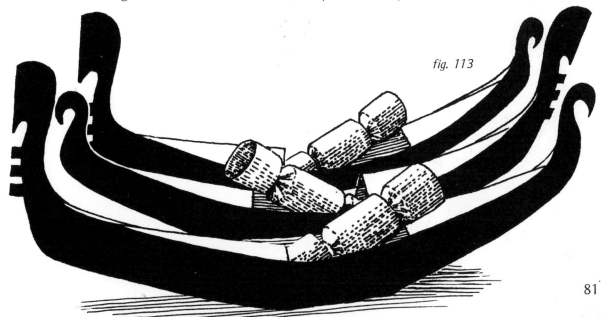

The Party Piece

Having described how to make, decorate and present your own crackers, I should like to suggest that you revive the tradition of making a theme for your crackers which runs through not only their outward appearance and presentation, but their contents as well. If flowers or gardening is your theme, your crackers can be made of flowered paper, presented as a floral display, and can contain packets of seeds and small bulbs with mottoes in the form of planting instructions. At a party at which games are proposed, charade crackers can help to get things going. The mottoes can give the word to be mimed with the help of the filling. Similarly, crackers can be used to pair together your guests by giving clues for partners.

fig. 114

9 Flowers

The essence of flower displays made for parties is that they should be striking and festive. Metallic surfaces, gold and silver sprays and glitter, which would over-dress an everyday arrangement, look well in artificial light and combine happily with dried plants, seed heads, paper and fabrics. Good results can be achieved very simply with a can of metallic spray paint and some dried plant material. Wheat, corn and barley collected in the summer, and seed heads from the garden such as delphinium and thistles are worth keeping and storing until you need them for your party. If you want to use dried materials when none are available in the garden, remember that many exotic dried plants are now imported and available from florists. If such dried plants are used as flower centres with feather or paper petals the results can be very successful.

If glitter is put on fir cones and leaves, use it selectively. I would much rather see few items well covered with glitter than the whole arrangement sprayed haphazardly. Attach glitter by sprinkling it on spray paint while it is still wet, or on to clear varnish, which shows the colour beneath.

Paper Flowers

Many papers and fabrics are suitable for making flowers for parties. Most smooth-surfaced or flocked papers are useful for leaves, with a wire glued on to give support and as a central vein, either underneath the material or between two layers. Decorative papers of all kinds can be adapted to make petals for flowers.

The most striking effects are often achieved by choosing contrasting materials for the flowers and the leaves.

Feather Flowers

Feathers can be used to make soft and delicate flowers. The small white fan-shaped turkey neck feathers (readily available around Christmas party time) are particularly useful for making trumpet-shaped flowers.

Feathers can be perfectly satisfactorily dyed by boiling them in fabric dye, and exciting effects can come from dipping just the tips of the feathers in a dye. It is not advisable, however, to spray feathers with metallic paint, which their delicate structure will not support.

Apart from turkey feathers there are many other kinds which can be used: goose, chicken, duck, pheasant, partridge and guinea fowl. Keep an eye on the poulterer's or the butcher's shop, and if you see an unusual fowl in the window ask the poulterer to keep some of the feathers for you. A handful of feathers will make a lot of flowers. As each feather has its own shape and curve very little preparation is required apart from sorting.

Before describing in detail a selection of simple flowers made from a variety of materials, there are some points worth mentioning which are common to all flower-making methods.

1. When making paper flowers, the base of the petals and the binding wire should be handled firmly, but not roughly — take care not to damage the petals at this stage.

2. When you cut petals for any single flower, cut them all together if possible, thus ensuring unity of size and shape.

3. Before you start to attach any petals, make sure that an

This display made entirely of silver flowers contains large cone-star flowers (p. 91) and frilly flowers of foil crepe with bead centres, sprays of lilies (p. 91) tinsel bulrushes (p. 92) and palm leaves (p. 92).

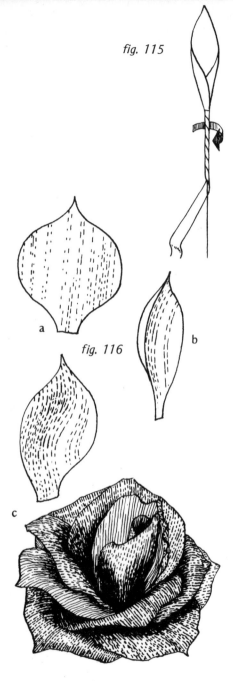

fig. 115

fig. 116

a

b

c

adequate length of binding wire is firmly joined to the stem wire, and use this piece continuously to bind in all the petals.

4. Bind all stem wires with an appropriate covering material. There are several alternatives available. Self-adhesive Gutta Percha, florists' tape made especially for the purpose, is the best but it is only made in a limited range of colours. Alternatively, crepe paper, available in many colours, can be used as a substitute simply by cutting a strip *across* the grain of the paper so that the crinkles will hold the binding tight. The whole of each stem should be bound by rotating it with the thumb and forefinger of one hand, and holding the binding material out in tension (fig. 115) with the other.

Rose

Materials Duplex crepe paper, stem wire and binding wire, binding tape.

Cut twelve petals each measuring 4 inches (10 cm) long to the shape shown in a, with the grain running the length of the petal. Divide them into two groups of three and nine petals. Shape the group of three petals according to b, by making a cup shape near the top of the petal, and the second group according to c, making a cup shape at the bottom of the petal and rolling the top part over. Take one of the petals from the first group and roll it up like a tube. Bind it tightly to the top of the stem wire with binding wire. Now add the remaining petals of the first group. Add four petals of the second group one by one, making sure that each one overlaps the previous one by half. Turn the remaining petals over so that the second colour is at the top, and add each petal separately as before. Bind the base of the petals and the stem. Crepe paper roses can be seen in fig. 13 on page 18.

Variations For Christmas decoration, foil crepe paper is most suitable (see Plate 4), but roses can be made equally successfully from single, double or glass crepe. They can be made to any size, the small ones requiring nine petals instead of twelve. The petals of single crepe paper roses dipped in melted candle wax have a translucent appearance, and this variation is very useful in flower arrangements. Miniature roses with petals 1 inch (2.5 cm) across make enchanting cracker decorations.

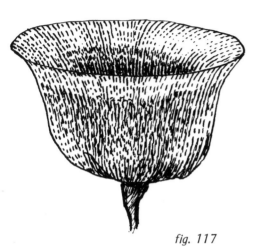

fig. 117

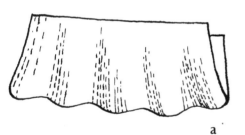

a

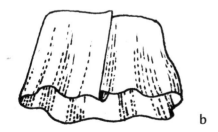

b

Foil Crepe Bells

Materials Foil crepe, stem wire and binding wire, binding tape.

Cut a piece of foil crepe measuring 7 x 4 inches (18 x 10 cm), with the grain running in the direction of the short side. Fold the piece of paper in half lengthways and frill all along the fold (**a**). Join the binding wire to the stem wire. Gather up the frilled crepe into a circle, tucking the end into the other end as shown in **b**. Attach this circle to the top of the stem wire and bind tightly with binding wire. Cover the base of the petal and the stem with tape to hide the join. Then ease the base of the flower out into a bell shape with the fingertips.

Variations These bells can be made in assorted sizes: single, double and in sprays with several bells to a single stem. An interesting combination can be made using two tones of foil crepe. This is another flower which is suitable for cracker decoration, particularly as it echoes itself the shape of the end of the cracker (see fig. 71). This bell flower can be adapted to look like a festive poppy if you make tinsel stamens from an inch (2.5 cm) of tinsel bound tightly to the top of the stem wire before the frilly crepe paper bell is added (see Plate 4).

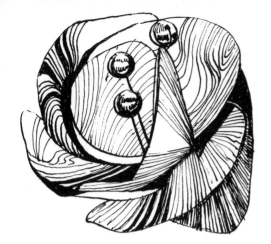

Melinex Flower

Materials Melinex, three beads for each flower, stem wire and binding wire, binding tape.

Make three stamens by threading each bead on to a piece of binding wire and twisting the end of the wire back on itself as shown in **a** (top). Then bunch the three together and bind them at different heights to the top of the stem wire. Cut five petals about 3 inches (7.5 cm) long to the shape shown in **b**. Assemble the flower by binding each petal separately around the stamens, first making a 'pleat' in the base of the petal to create a cup shape as in **c**. Make each petal overlap the previous one by half so that they are evenly spaced around the stem. Bind the stem with tape. (See Plate 4.)

Variations By varying the number of petals from three to seven this flower can vary from a bud to an open bloom. It can be made with many materials, and tissue paper is a good alternative to Melinex. If this flower is adapted for cracker decoration use one bead only for stamens, and keep the petals small.

Fir Cone Feather Flower

Materials One fir cone and six small feathers for each flower (guinea fowl feathers, black with white spots, obtainable from most poulterers, are the best), stem wire and binding wire, glue, glitter and spray varnish, binding tape.

Some fir cones are large, others very small. Ideal for this flower is a cone about 2 inches (5 cm) long, or as long as the feathers you propose to use.

Cover the stem wire with binding tape, make a hook on the top and hook it into the fir cone at a point where the scales start to open. Then spiral it down to grasp the base of the cone (**a**). Next spray the cone with varnish and dip it in the glitter.

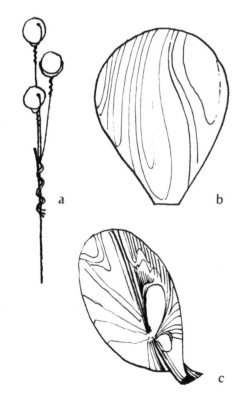

fig. 118

Then put glue in between two rows of scales around the centre of the fir cone and push the feathers in so that they curve backwards like an open daisy (b). This imaginary flower is very easy to make, and is quite stunning when used in large arrangements and with several layers of feathers.

Feather Daisy

Materials One seed head and six pheasant feathers for each flower, stem wire and binding wire, binding tape.

Almost any small seed head will make an attractive centre for this daisy, but it is helpful if the head you choose has a stem of its own so that it can be firmly attached to the stem wire with binding wire (a). Next bind on each feather individually, placing them evenly around the stem, so that they all curve outwards. Cover the base of the feather petals and the stem with binding tape.

Variations The size of the flower depends largely on the scale of your seed head. For small daisies a bead: gold, silver, pearl or coloured, is a satisfactory alternative for the centre.

fig. 119 Fir Cone Feather Flower

a

b

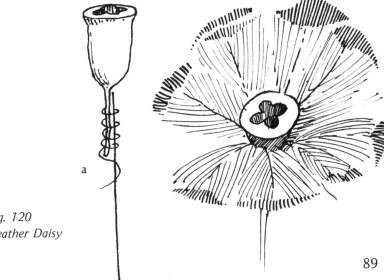

fig. 120 Feather Daisy

a

89

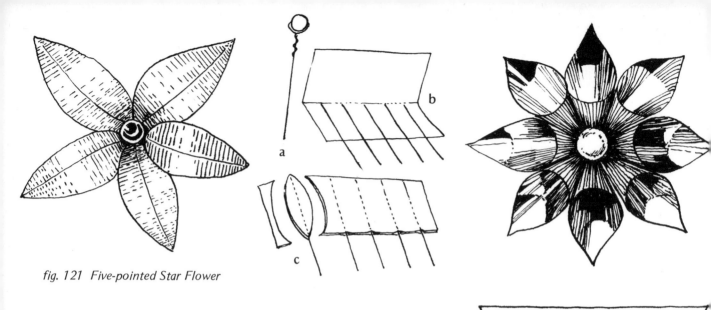

fig. 121 Five-pointed Star Flower

Five-pointed Star Flower

Materials Paper-backed foil, one bead for each flower, stem wire and binding wire, glue and binding tape.

Thread the bead on to a piece of binding wire, twist the wire together and then bind it on to the stem as shown in **a**. Make a fold in the paper-backed foil. Apply glue to the paper side and lay five stem wires on it up to the fold line as shown in **b**. Fold the paper over and press down firmly so that each wire stands out like a vein. Then cut out simple petal shapes as shown in **c**. Arrange the five petals around the bead and secure them to the stem with binding wire. Cover all the stem wires together with binding tape. The flower can be seen in the Wall Panel on page 18.

Variations This flower can be made to any size, and by varying the number of petals and beads the same flower can appear in many guises; for example, as a lily with six outward-curving petals and six beads at its centre (see the Festoon on page 16).

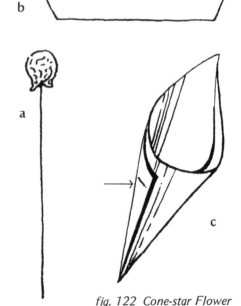

fig. 122 Cone-star Flower

90

Cone-star Flower

Materials Melinex, one puff ball for each flower, tin-foil, stem wire and binding wire, glue and Plasticine, binding tape.

First cover the stem with binding tape. Then apply glue to the top, push it into the puff ball and leave it to dry. Cover the puff ball with tin-foil by pressing the foil closely all round it as shown in **a**. Cut eight pieces of Melinex into the shape shown in **b**, the longest side measuring about 6 inches (15 cm) by 2½ inches (6 cm) deep. Curl each piece round to form a cone shape as in **c** and staple the cone into this position. Then staple the cones to each other in the position arrowed so that they form a circle, leaving a small hole in the centre for the stem. Use a little Plasticine to hold the petals to the puff ball.

Variations Paper-backed foil will serve as a substitute for Melinex, and a bead centre can be used for smaller flowers.

Spray of Lilies

Materials Paper-backed foil in two colours or textures, nine beads for each flower, stem wire and binding wire, binding tape.

Cut one of the stem wires in half, leaving the other one for the main stem. Thread each bead on to a piece of binding wire and twist them together in threes, fixing each bunch to the top of a stem wire as in **a**. Glue the contrasting paper-backed foils back to back, and cut three pieces about 3 inches (7.5 cm) long according to **b**. Coil each one around a bunch of beads and secure with binding wire as in **c**. Bind the stem with tape and assemble the spray by joining the three stems together so that each flower just reaches the base of the one below it.

Variations The lilies can be made and used separately as well as in sprays. Flocked paper backed with a foil paper makes an interesting combination.

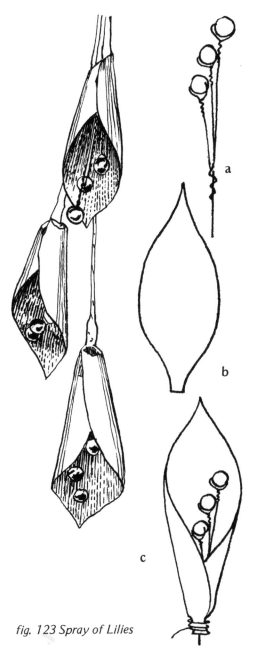

fig. 123 Spray of Lilies

Tinsel Bulrush

Materials Piece of tinsel 6 inches (15 cm) long, stem wire, binding tape.

First cover the stem wire with binding tape and then twist the tinsel around the top half of it in a spiral. If the tinsel you are using is made with a wire running through it, you can fix the ends simply by twisting the tinsel back on itself. If the tinsel you use has a thread centre, you must wire the ends to the stem with binding wire.

This simple shape is extremely useful in arrangements for Christmas. Very often a display made entirely of paper flowers needs softening, and these metallic bulrushes are a festive substitute for dried grass (see page 85).

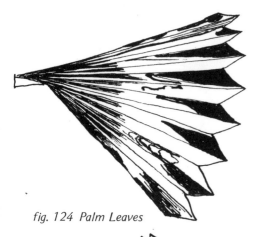

fig. 124 Palm Leaves

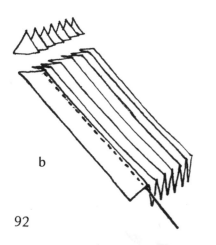

a

b

Palm Leaves

Materials Metal foil, stem wire, cellulose tape.

Cut a piece of metal foil about 8 x 6 inches (20 x 15 cm) and make concertina folds along its length (a). Press the concertina together and cut off the top corner to give the leaf a zig-zag edge. Attach the stem wire with cellulose tape to the first of the folds as shown in b, and tape the folds together at the base of the leaf. Then open out the whole leaf into a fan shape.

Variations Paper-backed foil will make a good substitute, although in this case care must be taken to ensure that the folds are crisp. If you use paper-backed foil, you have the choice of a wider range of colours.

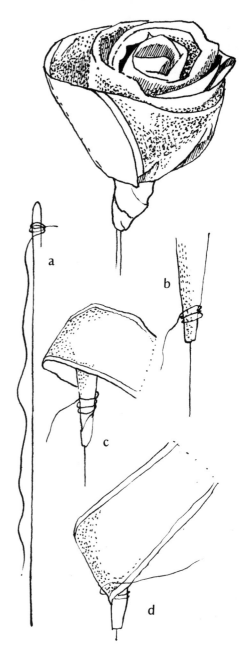

fig. 125 Ribbon Flower

Ribbon Flower

Materials A length of ribbon (preferably the kind with velvet on one side), stem wire and binding wire, binding tape.

Make a loop at the top of the stem wire and attach the binding wire as shown in **a**. Roll the end of the ribbon on to the stem, binding tightly with binding wire as in **b**. Fold the ribbon across the top of the stem, and downwards at an angle (**c**), catching and gripping the side of the ribbon with the binding wire. Take the ribbon upwards again, as in **d**, and when it reaches the top of the flower fold it over at an angle as shown in the finished flower. You will notice that the other side of the ribbon is now on the outside.

The key to making this pretty flower is to catch and bind the ribbon regularly at the base of the petals with binding wire and to fold the ribbon over to give a rose-like effect at the top of the petals. Repeat the process until you think the flower is large enough.

This velvet rose is not easy to make, but it is worth the effort. It looks well when accompanied by shiny foil leaves, and can also be made with parcel ribbon.

10　Gift Wrapping and Boxes

One of the aims of successful gift wrapping is for the parcel to disguise the contents. It is not always desirable to make a wristwatch look as though it is a bottle of wine or to wrap up a book in a hatbox, but it certainly adds to the pleasure of giving if not only the contents but the wrapping too comes as a surprise.

Gifts that have to travel through the post have their own problems, and the primary requirement here is stout protection, but for presents that are to be given at a party, the exterior of gift parcels can be decorated in the same way as crackers, using many of the same materials. A table which is so generously laid as to have a parcel as well as a cracker in each guest's place can look extremely handsome if the same colours and materials are used for both crackers and gifts.

Soft articles which are not damaged by crushing, such as socks, pullovers and scarves, can be squeezed into cardboard tubes or given a soft outer wrapping of tissue paper so that they can be shaped into a ball or any convenient form. There is no reason, however, why 'soft' presents should not be packed in firm-edged boxes like anything else. As a disguise, the candle-shaped box in fig. 126 was made for a scarf. The card cylinder was first covered with a piece of crepe paper large enough to be gathered in at each end before the top was decorated with a large cracker frill.

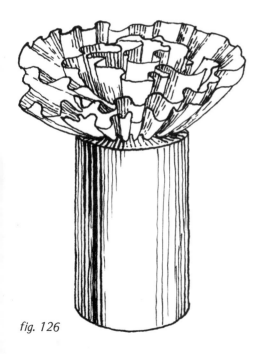

fig. 126

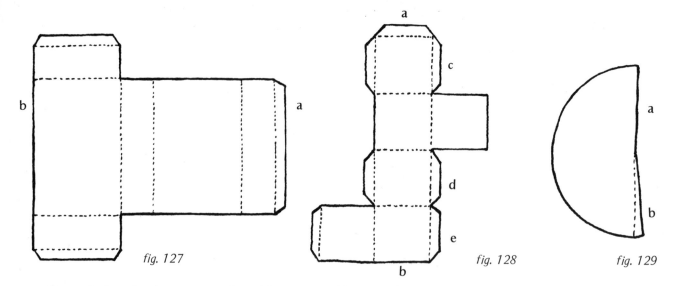

fig. 127

fig. 128

fig. 129

One of the simplest ways of making your gift wrappings distinctive is, of course, to re-cover existing boxes. Men's shirt boxes, for example, are a handy shape for enclosing other presents, as well as shirts, and they can be covered with a single piece of decorative paper tucked in over the lid. Once you have learned the simple technique of construction, however, you will find the greatest satisfaction comes from making boxes yourself to suit the gifts. Using cardboard, you can paste a patterned paper to one side with wallpaper paste if you want a box with an all-over pattern. Alternatively, you can decorate the different sides of the box in different ways.

The plans for a rectangular and a cube-shaped box are shown in fig. 127 and fig. 128. Cut the shape for the whole box from one piece of card wherever possible, as this avoids too many cumbersome joins. You will note that the diagrams include no measurements, since the size of the box is dictated by what you want to put inside it, and the contents will have to be measured carefully before you make your plan for the box. The cube box is easier, since only one measurement is required. Use a straight-edged ruler to draw up the plan on the card, and make sure that all the angles are right angles, or your box will look

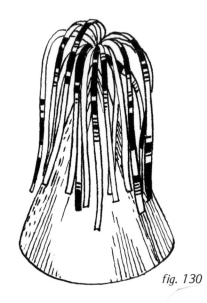

fig. 130

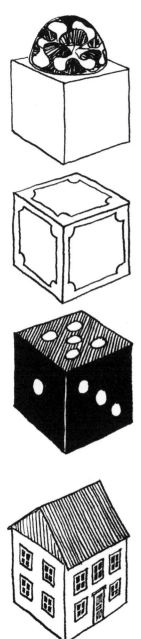

very strange when folded up. To complete the rectangular box shown in fig. 127 all you need to do is to glue **a** to **b**, and tuck the ends in. The cube box is assembled in the same way, by glueing **a** to **b**, although the base of the box is also glued to the tabs **c**, **d** and **e**.

A Cracker Box

To make a box to hold a dozen standard crackers, the rectangle forming the base of the box should measure 18 x 10 inches (46 x 25.5 cm). The sides of the box should measure a minimum of 1½ inches (4 cm) if the crackers do not have any form of frill or central decoration. If they do, then the box will have to be correspondingly deeper so that you do not crush the decoration.

Decorating the Box

Fig. 131 shows how a cube box can be wrapped or ornamented to suit special occasions or people. The top box is crowned with half a Melinex ball (see page 12). The middle designs have patterns drawn on the sides. The black box is made with black shiny card, sticking white labels on the sides like spots on dice.

To make a cube into a house as in the lower drawing takes time but can be a great delight to a child, who will almost certainly want to keep it intact. The roof is made with corrugated cardboard, and the doors and windows are painted on.

Basic geometrical shapes such as cylinders and cones are very striking. A cone can be made from cardboard cut in the shape shown in fig. 129. Once you have glued or stapled **a** to **b** and made a cone shape, stand it on a card to give the size of the circle you will need for its base. Add tabs to the outside of the circle so that you can fix it firmly to the inside of the cone with glue or tape once the gift is in. The finished cone, ornamented with a tassel on the top, is shown in fig. 130.

fig. 131

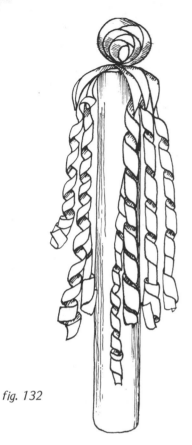

Once the box or wrapping is complete a extra decoration is often required. This can be provided simply with a ribbon, which may be necessary to tie up the box anyway, and a decorative bow. Many versions of a standard bow can be developed by adding more and more loops of ribbon as space allows, and the ends of stiff ribbons can be improved in appearance by being curled over a scissor blade into ringlets (fig. 132).

On a very simple box or plain wrapping paper it is tempting to be lavish with the decoration. You can add lace, beads and sequins, a spray of flowers, balls or anything you like, to make your parcel really distinctive. The decoration, however, does not need to be fussy, and some of the best gift boxes are ornamented simply with strips of contrasting material taped to the plain surface. The drawings on the facing page will, I hope, give you some useful ideas. Spots and stripes are quick to make and apply, checker-board and cut-out patterns are labours of love, but the result in each case is a box which looks too good to open.

You probably choose presents with great pleasure and skill, but I can assure you that they will be received with even greater pleasure if you spend a little time and care with their wrapping.

fig. 132

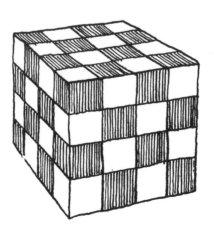

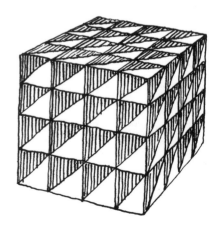

Sources of materials

The following specialist sources are invaluable for providing materials and tools to make the decorations described in this book.

Paperchase,
216 Tottenham Court Road,
London W.1.

for a great variety of papers, plain and decorative, including Melinex and acetate films

H.G. Kettle,
127 High Holborn,
London W.C.1.

for all kinds of papers and boxes, tissue, 'brick' and 'stone wall' papers, acetates

Gaiety Carnival Novelties,
Amen Corner,
Tooting,
London S.W.17.

for all cracker-making materials including formers, snaps, hats, mottoes, papers and gifts.

Stoneleigh Mail Order Co,
91 Prince Avenue,
Southend,
Essex

for all cracker-making materials, as above

Ells and Farrier Ltd,
5 Princess Street,
Hanover Square,
London W.1.

for beads, sequins puff balls, and perforated ribbon

All the other materials you require can be obtained from florists' shops (Oasis, Gutta Percha, binding and stem wires, dried plants, florists' ribbon), hardware stores (glue, spray paint, wire, dyes), stationers and (for feathers) butchers and poulterers.